SPACE OF LOVE

UNDERSTANDING THE POWER OF THOUGHT
AND WISDOM IN LIVING WITH AUTISM

GAYLE NOBEL

love & live
well!!

Phoenix,
Arizona

For information about this title or to order other books and/or electronic media, contact the publisher:
Nite Owl Books
11801 N. Tatum Blvd, Suite 143, Phoenix, AZ 85028
www.niteowlbooks.com
beverlyniteowlbooks@gmail.com

Library of Congress Control Number: 2018940821

ISBN: 978-0-9839702-8-6 (Trade Paperback)
         978-0-9839702-9-3 (E-Book)
         978-0-9998351-0-4 (E-Book)
         978-0-9998351-1-1 (E-Book)

Printed in the United States of America

Cover design: Christy Moeller, ATG Productions
Interior design: 1106 Design

Praise for

SPACE OF LOVE

Space of Love *brings a powerful message of hope to those living with* autism. *However, the message reaches far beyond that to anyone who, in the face of unexpected adversity and an uncertain future, has longed for a practical and profound path to living in the* Space of Love *more than they had dreamt possible.*

Gayle Nobel has written with gritty honesty, humility and wisdom about the bumps and potholes she has traversed, often more than once, on her journey. Believe me, you will not regret traveling with her and sharing the sights and insights she shares with you along the way.

—*William F. Pettit Jr., MD,* psychiatrist and student
and sharer of the Three Principles since 1983

Gayle Nobel allows us to enter the complex world of parenting an individual with autism on many exacting levels. Near the beginning she writes, "Resistance is the source of my stress, our stress as humans." That was enough for me to realize I had to learn more from this most wise woman.

This is a guide to the mindful parenting of exceptional individuals, with respect, insight and pure delight! Rainer Maria Rilke's work comes to mind. "Once the realization is accepted that even between the closest human beings, infinite distances continue, a wonderful living side by side can grow, if they succeed in loving the distance between them which makes it possible for each to see the other whole against the sky."

Gayle does exactly this for herself, for her family and for her son and now for us all. Her journey is all our journeys.

—*Raun Melmed, MD,* Co-founder and medical director,
Southwest Autism Research and Resource Center, director,
Melmed Center, and author of *Autism and the Extended Family:*
A Guide for Those Who Know and Love Someone with Autism

I found Space of Love *incredibly human, practical, wise, and extremely helpful for parents of children with autism. These personal stories of challenges that face any parent, especially the unique needs of autistic people, will guide parents toward trusting more deeply in their own inner source of wisdom and insight. The simplicity of "not knowing" and creating a space within for insight to fill the vacuum created, will be a relief to all who read and embrace Gayle's generous sharing of her life's journey.*

—*Joseph Bailey,* licensed psychologist and author of *Slowing Down to the Speed of Life, The Serenity Principle,* and many others.

Space of Love *by Gayle Nobel is an uplifting book for parents of children who are challenged by autism or other developmental issues. Sprinkled with ponderings and poetry about the parenting such a life requires, this book offers amazing insights. Sharing her positive mindset in a beautiful format, the author guides the reader to transform the weight of worries and runaway thoughts into affirmatives for a more joyful life. The author's inner wisdom resonates throughout the book, inspiring hope and nourishing the soul. This is a wonderful companion to her previous book,* Breathe.

—*Connie Hammer, MSW,* PCI Certified Parent Coach®, family consultant and author of *Autism Parenting: Practical Strategies for a Positive School Experience–Over 300 tips to help parents enhance their child's school success*

Space of Love *is a beautifully written book about our ability to live from a place that is deeper than intellect and logic: a space of love, where all is well and wisdom guides our actions. Through her touching stories and poetry, Gayle points us toward that space that is there at all times, even in the most challenging and uncertain of circumstances. I most highly recommend this book for anyone.*

—*Amy Johnson, PhD,* author of *The Little Book of Big Change: The No-Willpower Approach to Breaking Any Habit*

Space of Love, *Gayle Nobel's latest book, reflects the culmination of periscoped tension begun with her previous books,* It's All About Attitude *and* Breathe. *It is impossible to classify her work as poetry, prose or philosophy when one reads such beautifully crafted language such as "... the projector on the screen of our consciousness creating the movie called life." Gayle Nobel takes us on her journey and we, in turn, find our own vigorously enriched.*

— ***Rachelle K. Sheely, PhD,*** president, RDI
(Relationship Development Intervention)

Space of Love *invites the reader to go beyond the spectrum of autism and into the wisdom that lies within all. Though the stories are related to autism, the principles that underlie it pertain to all.*

— ***David Westerman,*** mental and performance coach

What a treasure! As in her other books, Gayle is able to share from her very heart and soul. Her courage in taking us on her journey through life with Kyle has no limits. One of my favorite questions from the book is, "What if you decide not to decide?" That's just one of the many tools that have become a regular part of my life through Gayle's insight and wisdom. This book is truly a gift.

— ***Tammy Kenyon,*** special education teacher

This beautiful and profoundly moving book is a gift to the world. Simple, honest and heartfelt truth on every page. I love the poems as well as the prose. It will be enormously helpful to anybody–not just parents, and not just parents of kids with autism. Highly recommended!

— ***Kimberley Hare,*** author of *The Heart of Thriving: Musings on the Human Experience*

Space of Love *is a simple and heartfelt read. It leads the reader to reflect deeply about the benefits of acceptance, trust, and living in the moment. You finish this book feeling a natural calm and a newfound confidence that life will be well, loving and living with autism. A beautiful and inspirational read.*

—**Kimberly Isaac-Emery, MSc,** autism specialist and family consultant

We often cannot see our own forests through the trees. Gayle reminds us to not only "breathe" but give ourselves a break. When our child was young, I wrote that "autism entered my life without permission and stole my peace." Now he is a man, and I realize that my peace has taken a different complexion. Sometimes peaceful, sometimes very sad, this is my reality. I have learned to brush myself off and count my blessings. He is our guiding force. When he soars, I fly. Resilience is the operative word. My first blog was coined resilientmom. I think I grew into the moniker, and I know Gayle gets this more than most.

—**Robin Hausman,** mom of son with autism

No one knows a child as well as a mother, and no one understands the demands on the mother of an autistic child like this mother, Gayle Nobel. Her dedication to her son Kyle has been marked by intelligence, creativity, and devotion. Her personal journey has taught her much. This book is her intent to share her achieved knowledge with mothers like her. Her suggestions are practical and caring. I recommend Space of Love *to every parent of a child with autism.*

—**Drake D. Duane, MS, MD,** Director, Institute for Developmental Behavioral Neurology/Biological Psychiatry, former associate professor of neurology, Mayo Medical School Rochester, Minnesota, and clinical professor of neurology, University of Arizona College of Medicine, Phoenix

To Neil, my husband, best friend, and love

FOREWORD

THE OTHER DAY, Gayle and I were texting back and forth about our sons and the current things that are going on with them. I asked her, teasing, "When is that manual coming out for us?" (You know, the one with all the answers to the questions that we've wondered about throughout all these years.)

Gayle wrote back, "Yeah, not sure. I think God is self-publishing, so it might be a while."

Smiling, I thought how easy it would be to have all the answers written out, and all I would have to do is open the book to that question and see the answer in front of me. Especially when it comes to the questions about my son and autism.

Gayle and I have been friends for almost thirty years, sharing our journey (mostly long distance) with our sons, who have autism. So often faced with challenges–many people would have just thrown in the towel. Gayle has never wavered in her devotion, passion and love for her son and her family.

Gayle opens her heart and soul, sharing her journey in three books. She offers sage advice, techniques and tools, with a keen insight, transcribed through poetry, essays and storytelling. Don't look now, but I think she has a direct line to the One who offers those answers.

This book is the latest in what I hope to see many more of in the future in her quest to write the 'answers' she receives from the Universe.

—*Kathy Almeida,* coauthor, *It's All About Attitude: Loving and Living Well with Autism,* and author, *Sunny's Story, Sunny's Story 2, And Then There was Rain*

INTRODUCTION

The Birth of
Space of Love

A FEW YEARS AFTER I wrote my second book, *Breathe,* published in 2010, I quietly decided it would be the last book. It looked to me like I had shared all I knew about living well with autism.

My message was that your attitude determines your experience. You can take an experience like parenting a child with autism and make it nicer, even easier, by putting a rose-colored lens on your camera. It is indeed possible to live a good, albeit challenging, life.

I encouraged readers to find the good and appreciate it. To do this, it's helpful to slow down and mindfully take one step at a time. Rather than trying to figure out how to balance it all, I suggested looking toward harmony. I emphasized making time for siblings and spouses and, most importantly, making time to take care of yourself, even in five-minute snippets.

This is a marathon, not a sprint, so taking care of oneself is essential for the health and well-being of the parent and caregiver, as well as the child. Rather than merely surviving, taking care of oneself looked like the key to thriving.

I offered a toolbox of tips and techniques from which to sample: things that seemed to help me on my personal journey. If one didn't resonate or work out, there was another one waiting on the next page.

I stepped out and spoke to parents, caregivers, and educators. As someone who lives it and gets it, I became an ear for moms. I offered a virtual hand or a virtual hug and, when possible, a real one. I sold books and even put my message on shirts. It's All About Attitude. Breathe.

Then one day, rather suddenly, it looked like it was time for me to move on to something new. I decided to step away from the autism world as well as the book business.

I set my sights on the question, "What's next for me?" For a while, all I heard was the sound of silence. I really didn't know. So I waited and kept my mind open while continuing my day-to-day care and life management of my son with autism, Kyle. With my daughters, Rachel and Leah, launched and living on their own, there was an empty space for a new passion.

After several months of exploring, I noticed a few breadcrumbs, followed them, and found myself signing up for a life coach training program. Hadn't I been doing something like that all along? It felt like a natural next step.

Fast forward past graduating from the International Coach Academy and starting a coaching business, only to discover something called "transformative" coaching. This was brand new to me and not previously on my radar.

I found myself walking off in a new direction, eventually leading to an online course called Living From the Inside Out. A few weeks in, during a conversation with the instructor, a coach, I had a tremendous personal insight about my relationship with Kyle.

As a result, I felt a new lightness and clarity. I experienced a deeper connection to my inner wisdom, as well as a new sense of freedom. Some of my internal suffering and struggle melted. All of this occurred during one conversation and it felt effortless. I wanted to know more.

A few months and many breadcrumbs later, I signed up for a transformative coach training program called Supercoach Academy, led by transformative coach Michael Neill. This program was based on the enlightenment experience teachings of Sydney Banks called the Three Principles. My understanding of the human experience was about to sail off in a new direction.

During my practice coaching hours, I connected with and coached some moms of kids with autism. My people. How about that? I had circled back home.

I discovered I now had something different to offer parents and caregivers. I was in new territory, well beyond what I shared in my first two books. As I continued to see where our experience of life really comes from, I was able to point others in that direction, too. As my own illusions began to dissolve, I saw new possibilities. In a very natural way, what I saw for myself spilled over into my conversations with clients.

My heart connection to those living with or working with people with autism or other special needs is my inspiration for *Space of Love*. The message in my stories extends to family, friends and anyone wanting to understand the experience of living with autism on a deeper level.

It is my hope that my personal insights embedded within each real-life story may serve as a spark to ignite some new insights for you, the reader.

Here we go. With love from me to you.

What If

DO YOU EVER PLAY the What If game with yourself? It may look like preparation, a way of solving problems or getting more out of life. However, it's actually an innocently created way of scaring ourselves with an imaginary crystal ball. It can appear and feel quite real.

It's filled with impossible-to-answer questions that often begin with What If or How. The voices in our heads can get rather loud and boisterous.

What if that happens? What if this doesn't happen? What if this never happens with my child? What if I can't do this? What if my child never does this or that? Or always does this or that? What if he gets stuck in this phase forever? What should I do about _____? What if I can't fix his autism? And finally, How am I going to figure this out, live with this, make it through this difficult, scary, rocky time?

I'm going to propose an antidote to this game. A spiritual salve. It's designed to be a catalyst to help you see that you don't need to even try to answer these kinds of questions. They may still pop up from time to time, but they don't require a lot of attention. This means straining and striving can take a back seat or even get out of the car.

What if you are connected to a universal energy that will guide you to wisdom every step of the way on this journey? This means you already have everything you need to figure things out, one step at a time. This guidance will help you know when to look to outside resources. It will also allow answers to spring from within, seemingly out of nowhere.

What if there is nothing to fix because innate resilience and well-being is the special elixir you and your child were born with? This means there is so much less to do. Stress and strain is optional.

What if you don't need a tool or technique to access well-being because it's always available beneath the surface of your busy mind? And when you settle, even for a nanosecond, you have the ability to dip into that space of peace, love, and clarity. This is because that space never goes away. It just gets obscured by busy, muddied thinking.

What if the stress and strain you feel is not coming from the condition of autism, your child's behavior or challenges, or the obstacles in your life? Your feelings are coming from your inside world rather than the outside world.

And finally, What if there's nothing to do about all of this because it's simply enough to know of it?

Ahh, this is all good news. The to-do list just got shorter. It may have even dropped to the floor for a moment.

If none of this is making sense right now, that's okay. Take a breath and read on.

Arrived

MY SON KYLE was born in 1983. For the first few months, he seemed like a typical baby. However, looking back at video, early on there were subtle signs that he was different. Something was off. The interacting and responding that is evident with very young babies was not quite there.

I didn't realize anything was amiss until he began having seizures at 5½ months of age. It was then that he received his first diagnosis. Epilepsy. By 18 months, autism. I had known for a while. It had been a fear of mine that I never said out loud.

Someone told me the best way to proceed was to love him, autism and all. Accept, be happy with, be okay with. See beautiful, no matter how different he was. Know he was okay and doing the best he could. As was I.

Confession: I couldn't do or see most of that. Not at all. I loved my baby deeply. My heart and soul hurt. I certainly didn't feel okay most of the time. I was filled with an unarticulated worry about the future. I don't think I admitted this to anyone, not even me.

I wanted to be in that place of acceptance. On the one hand, I dreamed of less internal struggle. On the other hand, I believed it was par for the course. A given when you had a child with autism. Don't give up. Fight, fight, fight.

Never give up but be okay with, even relax with, at the same time? Was that possible? Of course I saw beautiful when I looked at my baby boy, but it came with a "but." A big one.

I wanted to be in that place someday. A place of acceptance while at the same time, doing everything I could to help my son be the best he could be. I wanted to not want to fix him. I dreamed to know he wasn't broken. Different, yes, but not broken.

How would I get to this place within myself? I didn't know. I picked up my flashlight and shined it out onto the road. It was a dim bulb, only able to illuminate the next few steps. Off I went.

All I had was a direction in which to head. An intention of being okay with what was. Of knowing I was okay and he was okay and my family was okay. I gazed out toward someday. Not being able to see the future, "someday" was simply a blur.

During a recent interview, I had an insight. It slipped into my awareness rather quietly, without fanfare. Something new became clear to me.

I had arrived.

How long had I been here? I had no idea. It was not a moment, but a series of them. Moments, hours, days and years. It was more a gradual waking up than an actual arrival. One that I could not have predicted in any imagined future.

How did this arrival occur? Was there a method or technique? I have never tried to articulate this, but the answer seems simple now. I went about the business of living my life. I figured everything out as I went along.

Now I see–and this is a big thing to see–that that's all we can ever really do. Figure it out as we go. Put one foot in front of the other. Take one step and then the next. Live. Plan, but plan lightly. Because life takes place in real time. The rest of the stuff is in our heads or on pieces of paper.

I took many steps on many paths. Not linear, but zig-zagging all over the place, as life tends to do. At times the road was really rocky, the footing uncertain. At others, it was smooth and I could glide for a while. The full gamut of human emotions swirled in and out.

I lived my life. Because that's what was on the plate in front of me. No matter what thoughts were swirling around in my head, no matter what feelings were taking up residence in my body, there were things to do.

I celebrated victories, large and small. I laughed. I loved my children deeply. I made time for my husband.

I cried, too. I worried, making up stories in my imagination that never turned out to be true.

As humans, we have a propensity to make up futures, scaring ourselves with our predictions because we believe them. But the truth is, we are lousy predictors because people and situations are dynamic, not static. The future is unknown. And real life takes place in the moment, not in our heads.

My children grew into teens and now, adults. Life kept rolling along. I kept putting one foot in front of the other. Sometimes stumbling, even falling. Always getting up again, ever resilient. And I watched my children, including my son, do the same.

In the beginning, if someone would have told me I just needed to keep walking, one step and then the next, I would have dismissed it as too simple.

I never really needed a strategy for acceptance. My fearful thinking passed through without my help. Although sometimes I didn't *feel* okay, I always *was* okay. My circumstances could not take away my well-being. My outer world might be topsy-turvy and my thoughts stormy, but deep down below, there was a calm resolve, and resilience keeping my core solid: my default setting as a human.

With these insights, I came upon the sign I had been looking for.

You have arrived.

But keep walking, anyway. There's much more up ahead. It's called life.

When found, wisdom enhances the channels of the mind and acts like a penicillin for the soul.
> —Sydney Banks, *The Enlightened Gardner Revisted*

Resistance

AUTISM IS OFTEN symbolized by a puzzle piece. There's a search for missing elements that will yield a fix. Solutions.

I'm going to propose that the missing piece of the puzzle is something to notice and understand rather than something to fix.

Resistance. It's a common feeling and experience.

There is resistance against autism, an operating system that uses a different processor. There is resistance against the smaller picture, day-to-day things. My child is obsessed with _____. There is resistance against the bigger picture, overall quality-of-life things. My child is never going to have friends or be able to do _____. And there is a global, pervasive resistance to the entire autism package that colors our world at every moment.

It's resistance that actually creates our stress, unhappiness, and misery. Not our child. Not autism and what autism comes to mean for our child and our family.

I recently had a very powerful experience of the transient and thought-created nature my own resistance.

Kyle was sick. Shivering, under-the-covers sick. Flu and bronchitis knocked him out for a full week. It took him a while to bounce back to his energetic self and slip into the groove of his norm.

After the illness, he struggled with getting into the shower. It didn't look to me like he was afraid of the water or didn't want to be washed. There was something about positioning his body to step in, over the side of the tub. His reaction was one of sheer panic.

While trying to assist him, I felt tension within myself. Resistance. A resistance to his resistance. My thinking: "Oh, no, this can't be happening. He usually gets into the shower without issue. What if he never gets into the shower again? We need to get this done so he can be ready on time for his morning pickup. Not another obstacle!"

A swirling brew beneath my consciousness, the thoughts rolled on and on, fast and furious like a hailstorm. The more mental resistance I got into, the more stressed and tense I felt. I found myself trying to physically and verbally cajole him into the shower. Pushing.

Oh yeah. Pushing against his panic DOES NOT WORK.

There was a moment where I had the sensation of watching myself in a movie. I paused and took a step back. It was obvious we were not getting anywhere.

I found myself settling down. Just like that. Without effort. The thoughts blew through and I was left with a question. Now what?

How about Plan B?

I'm good at Plan B-ing. Plan B is obvious. I've done it before. Wash him out of the shower. Layer the floor with towels, get the

8

soap and do the job in an alternate location. He was fine with that. And after a moment, I was fine with it, as well.

When I settled down, I was able to hear what I knew. There is always another way. And in this case, the other way was a no brainer. Been there, done that. When I can listen beneath the static of my thinking, my inner GPS knows how to guide me. At first it's faint, and then the volume gradually increases to tell me what I know.

With my resistance out of the picture, I put Plan B into action. Everything flowed from there. Peace settled over both of us. We were able to get the job done with grace and ease and the results were good enough. Hair washing would wait for another day.

Later on, an insight popped to the surface of my awareness. Resistance is the source of my stress, our stress as humans.

That's right, resistance. Not my child. Not his behavior or abilities. Not the label of autism.

I kind of knew this already. But it was as if I rode the elevator up a few more floors and saw it in a new way, on a deeper level.

Resistance, arguing with what is, shows up as a feeling. And not typically one that feels good. Stress, anxiety, worry. And much more. We feel it in our body. It can adversely affect our health. It paints our reality.

But here's the thing. And it's a really, really big thing. Resistance is made of the energy of thought. Resistance = Thought.

Thoughts create the argument with what is. They push back. They kick and scream. "He CANNOT be having trouble getting in the shower. He always gets in the shower. Why do simple things have to be so hard? Still!"

When I am in resistance, it's like someone has put a sack over my head. Old, stale thoughts repeat themselves like a broken record. I don't see or hear anything new. It feels like I'm stuck.

Thoughts appear solid. They paint a picture of reality. Just like a movie, I'm drawn into the story 100 percent.

I can't force myself to stop being resistant. That looks like even more resistance. However, eventually I wake up. The storm passes. The lights go on in the theater. The thoughts fade, making room for a new batch. Wisdom and intuition blow in.

And there, right there, is the fresh energy of Plan B. Shiny and bright like an "a-ha." Or perhaps a "duh." Possibly something I've done before but looking brand new to me in the moment. Suddenly, reality looks completely different. A new movie.

At some point, I see resistance for what it is. Without effort on my part, it eventually melts in the sunshine of my understanding. In its place is direct access to my innate well-being, the space where wisdom flourishes. I remember my ability to figure out how to make things work. Good-enough solutions suddenly appear like a washcloth and a bar of soap in the middle of the bathroom.

Suddenly, my desire to control dissolves and gives way to a fresh understanding. Kyle and I get on with our day. And our lives. Not the one in the "how it should be" box. But the one that takes place in real time.

Autism, to me, is not a mental illness. It describes a person with a brain (computer) with a somewhat different processor than the majority of people. The mind, however, is connected to the same spiritual source. Each person, regardless of their processor, knows the experience of Love and Joy and the innocently created experience of stress and turmoil.

—Dr. Bill Petit

LEMONADE

A child with Autism
When you tell people, they seem sad
a momentary gaze of pity crosses their face
Beyond compassion, sympathy perhaps

Life gave you a lemon, say their eyes
"He's so handsome though"

A lemon
Something to deal with
An obstacle to happiness and a good life

Something to reframe
Put a new lens on the glasses
from which you gaze out into your world

Make the best of it if you can
Squeeze that lemon, add sugar
Make lemonade
The only way to make it okay

But what if...

the lemon-ness of autism
is not real
but made of thought?

And our experience
does not come from our child,
his behavior, his autism
but from lemony thoughts.

They create our lemony experience.

What if we have the ability
to allow the energy of thought
to float through,
knowing there is something new
that will come along?

Something sweeter
at any moment in time

Nothing to do but wait
live
notice
and love.

The transient nature of thought
creates the transient nature of our experience

Yes, transient

We can see something new
without effort
or
fixing
or
doing
or
changing our child

No squeezing of lemons
because lemons don't exist

They are not solid like the ones on my tree
They are made of the formless energy of
thought

A relief to know I don't have to fix my son,
so handsome
or my experience,
so fluid

Or make a single glass of lemonade

Decisions

LIFE IS FULL OF decisions. Have you noticed decisions can appear magnified when you have a child with autism? No matter the age of the child, the decisions can feel as if they are living, breathing and rushing toward you at record speed. There are so many!

You seek solutions, and thoughts rev up, moving faster than the speed of life. Pretty soon there's a feeling that your head might just explode if you have to decide on one more thing. A perfect definition of overwhelm. Mix in a few spoonfuls of fear, and we have innocently created that uncomfortable feeling of stress. It's not particularly shiny, pretty or inspiring. It feels complicated rather than simple.

The decisions often wear the facade of really big mountains to climb. Huge. They come in many flavors and often have the fragrance of urgency.

How do I connect with my child when he doesn't respond in the typical ways? How do I teach my child when he doesn't appear to learn in the typical ways? Medication, doctors, therapy, schools? Interventions, strategies, solutions, answers?

Personally, I often entertain the mother of all questions/decisions. Where will Kyle live when he doesn't live at home?!? Who will be his main support when I am no longer here?

There are so many pieces to the quality-of-life puzzle for my child and family. Big questions can seem as if they have to be answered right now or even yesterday. And once answered, there are usually many more piled up in the wings waiting for solutions.

Kyle is not verbal. So I go by keen observation and intuition. There are so many unknowns with him.

A basic one is when it seems as if he might be sick. Or perhaps he is just out of sorts and tired. Should he stay home? Should he go to the doctor? Should he take some medicine? Yes or no. Yes or no. And then after the yes or the no is answered, more questions.

More choices and decisions. The thoughts create a mental flood and I have the sensation of drowning in overwhelm. Overwhelm is when my thoughts are moving faster than the speed of life. And I can't stop them. They rock and roll on their own accord.

Until they settle, which eventually they do. Again, on their own accord. I pop my head above the water. Seems drowning was an illusion after all. A trick of the mind. I can breathe again.

My daughters without autism are able to make their own decisions now. They are adults. They might want an ear or a sliver of advice, but they decide for themselves. Choose A or B, go right or left.

Kyle does not get to decide on most things. He can't communicate for the big decisions. He doesn't seem to have the judgment or awareness of the options and their implications. Though I'm sure he knows and understands more than it appears, so much is unknown. By default, he has handed his decisions over to me.

Decisions used to feel really heavy. This way or that. Pros and cons. Should I or shouldn't I? Sometimes elevated to life or death by the repetitiveness and speed of my thoughts. Then I saw and deeply understood something really big.

My inner wisdom. A personal GPS run by the power of intuition.

It might be experienced as a sense we get or a gut feeling. It feels like a connection to something larger than myself. Yet at the same time, it feels like a deeper part of myself. Even when I forget or can't see or hear it, I know I am always plugged into this guidance system. An invisible and powerful friend at my side or on my shoulder.

In hindsight, I can see my intuition has been my guide even when I barely knew I had a guide. Now that I can see and feel it more clearly, I know I don't have to work so hard at decisions.

I ran an experiment one day on something small and inconsequential. What if I decided not to decide? What? But hmmm. And waited until I knew. How would I know? Would I just know? What would that feel like?

I set off on a hike. I usually plan my route. There are several choices along the way and they take different amounts of time. A little pre-hike mental rehearsal always tells me where I will be going. But what if I didn't make a plan, rehearse the route? Decide not to decide. And at each juncture, listen for what I know. Because it didn't matter which way I chose. No right or better way.

What I saw was at each intersection in the trail, I knew which way to go. Without reasons, pros and cons, plans, I knew which way to turn. I didn't even need to stop and consider the options. I flowed with the direction I knew to walk.

But life is not that simple, you say. Decisions regarding our kids have consequences. Some are better than others. Yes and maybe. I'm starting to see that it is much simpler than I ever imagined.

We have no way of really knowing on what path each choice will take our child, where it will actually lead. Though we act like we can orchestrate it, the future is unknown.

And the pro-ing and con-ing, and agonizing and futurizing and deciding and undeciding serves as noise in our systems. At times, fast and furious. And pretty soon, we feel overwhelmed by this noise.

Our connection to intuition lies beneath all that static. It is always there. Always. Because it is built into the human operating system.

The noise and busy-ness in our heads may drown it out, but eventually, something will get through. We will hear or see something. Or simply know to do something or talk to someone. We are always capable of knowing the next step. We just forget, believing we need to work or think harder to find it. The opposite is actually true.

There have been some big decisions for Kyle. And yes, sometimes my thoughts have shaded them the color of life or death.

There have been many times when I felt lost for the next step, where to turn. And then something appears, tapping me on the shoulder. Psst, look over here. Or, walk this way. It's subtle, a whisper. Or a middle-of-the-night awakening, loud and clear like a brass band marching in my awareness.

A fresh idea. My eyes light up and I know the next step. A decision looks obvious. No longer lost, I see something I didn't see before. Carrying the scent of inspiration, a shiny new insight emerges. I decide.

The design of the human system seems to be that our common sense and deeper wisdom work best when used together. The wisdom of our deeper mind guides our way forward whenever we let it, without ever trying to take away our free will.

—Michael Neill, *Creating the Impossible*

SPACE OF LOVE

I groan
Yet another early morning
I'd rather roll over and sleep

But he awaits.
My job begins early,
before the crack of dawn, at times.

Shower, shave, brush teeth
and more
Only with help.
Mine

Whereas most people do this on their own,
effortlessly
Not Kyle.
A fact.
It is just this way.
No judgment
Not any more

There is something about this space
This space we share in the groggy mornings
silently, sometimes
or with chit chat, sometimes
our chit chats
Beating to the sound of an unconventional drummer

Each day similar
Yet brand new
We show up differently to each other
and the tasks at hand
And to this space

I check in.
I know how his day begins
in connection with mine
I like knowing and connecting
I soon forget
how early it is

Others say out loud
Or silently
"Why not get someone else to do this job?
Anyone could do it."

I now see why I still do.

No
not anyone could show up
And be in this space of love

There is something about it

Others think burden
But they don't get it

I'm drawn in
There's still something here
for me
for him
for us

The space beyond the words
and into the feeling
The space that is us
And at the same time,
Is much more than us

What we are all searching for
something intangible
esoteric even
Solid yet formless

Space of Love

Space

of

Love

Grit and Grace

KYLE GOES THROUGH severe rough patches we call "cycles." He experiences regular episodes of intense anxiety and agitation. His behavior and demeanor change dramatically. His appetite disappears. These cycles show up and hang around for a while, showing up every two weeks and lasting two weeks. It looks a bit like a different person takes over Kyle's body. Cycles are an add-on to his already challenging autism.

Eventually they stop and don't appear for nine months or a year or five years. Sometimes the stopping is because we tried something and maybe it helped. Or perhaps they just stop because it's time.

They've been a part of our lives for more than twenty years, but each time he goes into one, there is an element of surprise. Though their timing pattern is predictable, their onset is sudden.

Life changes dramatically. Kyle's world becomes small, as he is confined to the house. Our focus is on his health, safety and comfort.

We have a system of sorts. As does Kyle. In many respects, he knows what to do. Though it looks baffling to us, he has an extreme way of taking care of himself. His own inner wisdom with his unique way of expressing it.

I've had a lot of different stories about these cycles.

I used to float down the river of misery, kicking and screaming and feeling sorry for all of us. I described them as debilitating, stealing his life, hijacking his soul. Poor Kyle. Poor us.

These days, I notice much less of a story. The cycles are part of Kyle's life until they aren't. We all do the best we can to live with them.

I still get fooled, but more often I see the stories for what they are. And the heaviness I used to feel has lightened. This isn't to say I don't sometimes feel frustrated or upset or sorry for him and for all of us. But my story feels less solid and much more fluid than it used to. And with this, my feelings seem more fluid, as well.

Sometimes I just sink into the moment with him. Allow intuition to show me what to do next and next and next. With less angst and more flow, I discover a deeper space of love and compassion. From this more relaxed, even creative place, solutions appear.

GRACE

Sometimes I'm in resistance and fight mode. I flex my muscles, put my superhero suit on, and go about analyzing and doing stuff to fix his pain. I get stuck in repetitive thought loops. Errrr. Struggle. Swimming against the flow is hard, exhausting work.

GRIT

Two weeks pass, and the cycle is over. Grace and grit are replaced by a rush of gratitude.

My son, once again, appears to be at peace. He is able to go out and participate in life. It feels nice to be grateful. Enjoy the ordinary moments that I see aren't really ordinary at all. I release the breath in the places I was holding it.

I see now that I don't need to try to force gratitude, to work at it until I feel it. I can be with myself where I am. Even when it feels gritty. This looks like grace. I am also able to be with my son where he is, even if he's in pain. More grace.

From a state of grace, gratitude is only one thought away.

The only trick in life is to be grateful for your highs and graceful with your lows.

—George Pransky

RESILIENCE

Like a tree in the wind,
he sways.

First a little
then a lot
Suddenly the wind turns wild, a storm now

Branches move, crackle, and break
Falling to the ground
Even the thick trunk is shaking

He is in the grips of a cycle
an inner force, a storm,
that throws him this way and that
from the inside out

If he had branches and leaves,
they would drop

The wind can't be stopped
by the tree
or my son
or I

It stops when it stops.

And somehow,
he knows what to do during the storm
I see that now
I didn't before

Curl up
rest
sit
pace
Stay in the groove of a fixed pattern of movement
Don't let us take off the item which protects him

Deep in his core, his trunk
he is okay
Shaking in the wind
but okay on the inside
Nature's design of trees and humans

The tree is resilient,
its trunk, solid
despite what the branches and leaves are doing

You can chop it down
or even burn it
There is a good chance it will still sprout and grow something.

Because that's part of the design of trees
to bounce back, despite wind and humans
Resilient naturally

Kyle, resilient naturally
Me, resilient naturally

Bouncing back
as if there never was a cycle,
a storm
As if it never happened

Better than ever
new sprouts, limbs, leaves
Growth, big and small

Resilience
an innate part of the design
The default setting of trees and humans
including me and my son.

I Don't Know

ARE YOU AFRAID OF these words? Do you hesitate to say them? Silently to yourself or out loud? Or to others?

It can almost feel like a weakness, this "not knowing" business. Not knowing what to do or how to move forward. Not having a solution to something. Not knowing where you want to go or how to do something. Our egos get a little weird at the mention of those three words, *I don't know.*

Recently, it was the day of my daughter's birthday and I still didn't know what to get her. I wanted to make it special in some way as it was a birthday ending in zero.

I was sitting in the I Don't Know space but it didn't feel very spacious. It was packed with thought, including worry. What if I didn't come up with anything by the time she came home for Thanksgiving?

My method ...

Think hard and think some more. Nothing. Google search for ideas. Nothing. Think again. Nothing. Ask other daughter.

Something, but no, not it. Think. Rehash previous ideas I didn't like. More nothing. Errr, figure this out. Sigh.

And then ...

I was in the parking lot of the grocery store. I had temporarily forgotten my search for the ideal milestone birthday idea. Out of the blue came something new. A brand new idea, straight from the divine creative soup in which we all float. It actually came with sort of an energetic whoosh. Suddenly the I Don't Know space was filled with something shiny and fresh. I knew it was what I had been seeking.

I had three days to complete the brilliant birthday project. This awareness shot me right back to the I Don't Know space. I didn't know how I would get it done in such a short amount of time. I didn't even know what most of the items would be. However, I had what I needed. I knew I could put one foot in front of the other and figure it out, one item at a time.

Not knowing turned out to be my friend. It seemed to unleash a fresh creative flow. Little by little, ideas trickled in. One idea seemed to open the way for the next one. Within three days I had everything I wanted to create a special basket of thirty gifts.

What about "serious" things? What about when I don't know what to do about something that looks like a really big problem? For example, Kyle's severe and intense cyclical episodes. He tends to break through remedies after using them for a while. We often find ourselves on the search for what to try next to calm these cycles.

The last time this happened, his doctor was at a loss. It looked as if we were at the end of the road. Out of options with nothing left to do. At a low point, I didn't know where to look or who to ask. "I don't know. I REALLY don't know," I shouted silently to myself.

Not knowing was not where I wanted to be. An avalanche of scary thoughts about the future left me feeling discouraged and fearful. Until I saw something.

I don't know might actually be useful. It's difficult to get through to someone who already thinks they know everything. What if I Don't Know actually makes space?

The space is not filled up with what I already know. Or what I *think* I already know. It is filled with what? Essentially nothing. From this place, I noticed I was actually quite open and willing to hear something new.

And then ...

I was given a lead by someone who has been in my Kyle's life for twenty years. She went out of her way to help. And by following a few breadcrumbs, she got the name of a doctor with expertise in my son's issue. Feeling hopeful, I took this lead and ran with it.

Two weeks later, my husband and I found ourselves on a two-hour Skype call with a doctor across the country. He came up with nine new potential solutions, some that could be combined with each other to make even more. We were left with a few years worth of options from which to pick and choose.

Out of nothing left to do came a long list of options. One doctor didn't know. But the next one did. I didn't know. And then I did.

I'm starting to see something about not knowing. It's not my enemy. It's my best friend. It creates space. And that space is available for possibility. It's fertile ground for new ideas, insights, and solutions to come through. An infinite well.

So let's hear it for I Don't Know. Let's shout it out and then get ready for the rain of fresh ideas to come down. Maybe one drop at a time. Or possibly a downpour. Within that rain can be something fresh and new. A next step. An idea. Something to see, know, or do.

I Don't Know. I kinda like the ring of those words now.

You can't solve a problem with the same level of thinking that created it.

—Albert Einstein

What If It's Not a Choice

I HAD A THOUGHT STORM while watching news reports about the terrorist attack at the Brussels airport. We flew out of that airport the previous summer. I was going to be flying to London for coach training in the near future. A gust of fearful thoughts blew in. Worry and fear built a knot in my stomach. And fear led to more thinking in the form of questioning whether I should ever leave my house again because I could be in danger. Thoughts linked together to create a saga. And my saga looked and felt very real. As real as the explosions in the airport. For the rest of the evening, I was caught up in it.

I was halfway into the next day when I realized the thought storm had blown through. Although world events hadn't changed, my thinking had moved on to other stuff. In fact, the thought energy of the previous night and the fearful feelings weren't even on my radar. Without any help from me, something big happened on the inside.

New thoughts = new feelings = new perception of reality.

Thoughts blow in and out like the wind. They literally show up out of nowhere. Sometimes they appear associated with an event and sometimes they seem random. And although I'd like to believe I have control over them (think positive, think positive), I notice they tend to flow through or hang around, and then leave in their own time.

Have you ever had someone (maybe you) advise you to just "let it go"? And as hard as you try, you just can't do it? Yeah, me, too.

Letting thoughts go on command hasn't worked too well for me. In fact, sometimes the effort involved in letting them go has backfired and the thoughts have repeated so many times they get even louder and feel even more solid. Real. It looks to me like giving them a dose of extra attention, or love, has actually kept them hanging around. And then I pile some judgment on myself (more thinking) for not being able to let them go. As if letting them go would be a better, more "enlightened" choice.

But what if it's not a choice?

Like the wind and clouds, thoughts are fluid. Some of them are below the surface of our awareness and we don't even realize they are there. Under the radar, they're filtering through consciousness to create our perception of reality.

Some of them show up in the form of chatter. We hear them loud and clear. They might be fleeting or repetitious. We may believe them or we may not. Linked together, and repeated, they create stories about our world and who we are. They can seem solid. Hail or ice instead of wind and clouds.

Some thoughts are fresh and new. Insights, a slice of inner wisdom coming through our consciousness. And suddenly, we see a new reality and it appears as though everything has changed even though the outside world is still the same.

When the thought storms settle, the insights have a way of slipping in. A fresh cookie emerges from the metaphorical oven of the universe. Something from nothing. Insights may come in as a whisper or a tap on the shoulder. Or they come in with a big bang. An OMG moment. Insights sound exciting. I think I'd like to choose to have more of these.

But what if it's not a choice?

Recently, upon waking, my husband randomly came up with a brilliant insight about what to do with our broken pool filter. Insight and pool filter may seem like an unlikely combination. But an insight is simply a brand new, fresh thought. Sometimes an answer to something that looks like a problem. It may or may not be spiritual or deep. One minute my husband was going from sleep to awake and mumbling a groggy "good morning," and the next, he was a pool repair genius. He didn't have the luxury or pressure of choosing that insight.

What I'm seeing more clearly than ever before is that we don't choose. Our thoughts are not in our control. I must confess, I'm a bit blown away by this. It turns quite a few of my long-held beliefs upside down. But since beliefs are made of thought, they dissolve when they don't look true anymore. And I don't even have to do anything with them.

What I love about this is that it takes the pressure off and helps soften the judgment. If I can't control the fact that I'm making my grocery list during yoga class, I'm free to hang out wherever I'm at until the next batch of thoughts roll in.

I'm free to choose to take action. Or not. I've yet to decide to run out to the grocery store in the middle of yoga. And without effort, my grocery list eventually floats away. Sometimes I'm left with some empty space for a while until the next batch flows in.

There is a great freedom in knowing it's not up to me to fix my thinking and that I don't need to work really hard to let something go.

In understanding the transient nature of the energy of thought, I see that I don't need to believe everything I think. Or act on it.

There's no such thing as a solution to a feeling.

—Michael Neill

THOUGHT PAINT

Thought
The paint creating our human experience

sad
&
happy

stressed
&
relaxed

worried
&
joy filled

and everything else

Emotions created from thought, not the situation
Not the person I brought into this world
Not even his label, the description of his differences

Looking back ...

My consciousness, the paintbrush,
Used thought, the paint
To create scary pictures of the future
And I believed them

I didn't know I didn't have to
I didn't know they were made of energetic clay
which humans use to sculpt automatically
without knowing they are sculpting

I was not yet on to the illusion
that thoughts are not solid
not reality
not even created by me

They blow in and out
and in and out

Many unwanted and not in my control
I try to corral and manipulate them
Think this way, not that way

Like diverting a stream with some rocks
It works only briefly, if at all,
until the rocks get swept away by the flow

Thoughts
They sneak in the back door

What if
what if
what if
They ask over and over
Like a song
I can't get out of my head

Painting and painting and painting their pictures
on the canvas of my mind
Feeling so real
in my head
in my heart
in my belly
So real, they make my body hurt
Their song, made up
Technicolor pictures of the future
MADE UP!
Made up? By who?
Can't be me because I am the one listening

Thoughts
not real, not solid
but so powerful, they change my physiology

Thought energy,
Invisible
Affects physical energy, brain chemistry
Amazing we humans are

Getting scared
Dreading what is coming
5,10,15, 20 years from now
when Kyle is 10, 15, 20, 25

Afraid of the thoughtmares,
I didn't know I could and would
wake up and turn on the light
The thoughts would pass, and for a while,
the paintbrush would rest in the sink
The canvas, once again blank

A new set of paint colors, always available
flowing through from the endless supply of paint

I saw his face, asleep in my arms
Jolted awake from my scary thoughtmare

I saw love
I sensed all was well.
He was well and I was well
In that moment

Isn't that all we have?
That moment
Then that one and that one
and that one

Fresh paint, always within reach
Clean brushes
New canvases
Connected to something greater than ourselves

I saw that in him
And in me

Change

PEOPLE WITH AUTISM don't like change. My son/daughter does not like change. Hates it, in fact. So do I. Change is hard. Change is stressful. All of this is so widely accepted, it's considered common knowledge.

Life is all about change. In fact, life itself is change. It's always in a state of flow. From one moment to the next, one day to the next, the energy of life is in motion. Sometimes it seems slow, others fast. It may look stagnant until we look deeper. It may appear like a high-speed train, until our minds slow down.

Like a river, there is an ebb and flow to life whether we are in a state of flow with it or are paddling against the current. We can muscle through or we can ride the flow, steering where we can. Ultimately, we aren't in charge, and periodically, we're bound to hit what we might consider boulders.

At this time, the scent of a big change is all around me. I'm in a familiar place similar to ones I've been at before, yet it feels different this time around.

Once again, I'm looking for a caregiver for Kyle. Yet another new person to bring into his life. This time it's not because his current person is not working out or we don't like her or she is moving on. She has a health issue that is uncertain. She will probably be back, but we don't know when or in what capacity. Time to be proactive before she takes her leave.

I sit in what feels like the great unknown, the empty space from which new possibilities bloom. I throw a few seeds out into this space. Water it a little. Take a few actions. Talk to some people who can help. Sign up to a caregiver website.

I begin pointing my laser in the direction of what I'm looking for. For right now, that's all I have. A direction. And even though I've been down this road many times before, the direction is brand new.

I used to get scared when I was in this position. Almost panicked at times. Even resentful. I rely so heavily on the people in Kyle's life, especially when someone has been with us for so long and has become a part of our family. There is ease and trust that builds up over time. Will we have that again with someone else?

I have come to see that my options are not limited. New people are always coming into the field of possibilities. Another person will come along. And she will bring new things to Kyle's life and to ours. Things I haven't yet imagined. Trust and ease will build over time.

Change. It's the one thing we can count on. Change is built into the fabric of life. We see it in nature. We see it in people. We see it in our bodies. We see it in the big picture as well as the small details.

We meet change with such resistance or fear. Holding back change can be like trying to stop the rain. Or the leaves from falling. Or a baby from being born. Or lifting a hundred-pound bar over our head.

We act as if the stress of lifting that bar is just par for the course and built into change. When actually it's change that's built into us, into life. The bar isn't real. The stress is only made of our resistance. Our resistance is always made of thought. Thought is formless energy.

Change is good. Change is stressful.

Change is neither.

Change is.

And then we make it mean something. Something bad or good or scary or exciting. Thought might grab onto an upcoming change and go to battle with it. Or embrace it.

Inhaling the energy of big change, I feel light around the edges and calm at the core. Not my usual. I know I will figure it out as I go, one step at a time, because that's all I can do, anyway. Suddenly, I sense simplicity.

I sit at the edge of this piece of life's garden. It looks rather barren right now. I know those seeds I've tossed into place lie just beneath the surface. Some will sprout and some will not. There is growth and movement that is not yet visible to my eye. And it is not entirely up to me.

Yes, this project is not up to me. There is a connection to something larger than myself. A universal force working behind the scenes. I like that I'm not completely in charge. This understanding is where my power lies.

I've done my part of the job. I've planted. I will keep showing up to tend the garden, watering and feeding. Taking steps, yet
resting in the unknown. A place of possibility.

*No man ever steps in the same river twice, for it's not the same
river and he's not the same man.*

—Heraclitus, Greek philosopher, born 544 BC

HELLO LIFE

Hello Life
I have a dilemma
I don't know what to do about this and that
And that and this

I've been thinking a lot
Thinking and thinking some more
Wracking my brain for a solution
Pro-ing and con-ing

How can I help Kyle with this?
And that too.
It looks like I must figure this out with my little brain
I must hash it out with sweat, tears, and effort
A large dose of it.

I feel overwhelm, frustration, and strain
My head is busy with lots and lots of striving
After all that, I still don't have an answer

I keep searching the computer files of my little-m mind
only to come up with the same stale solutions
Old news, dated files

Reluctantly, I admit defeat
Throwing up my hands, I give up
I have to
I have nothing
I am empty
It appears I have exhausted all possibility

Until ...
I'm driving along listening to music
And I receive a download
From big-M Mind
the universal intelligence to which we are all connected

It comes in quickly and with ease,
lacking fanfare
A group of ideas in rapid succession

A Big One at the beginning
and some ideas on what to do with it at the end

WOW
Insight express!
Without effort and strain

This download is filled to the brim
With fresh insights
Containing new options and directions

Reminding me that the possibilities
are infinite
even when I can't see them
Or imagine what they could be

In giving up,
I left a message for life
And sure enough,
Life got back to me

Delivering a fresh bundle of ideas
newly plucked from the tree of possibility

Hello Life
and
Thank You

It's Raining

I WAS IN THE MIDDLE OF a thought storm. It ran the gamut from a heavy downpour, to a moderate steady flow, to a light drizzle. Without an umbrella, I felt very emotional and vulnerable. Just when it seemed as if the rain might stop and I could breathe again, I was pelted by a new stream, even stronger than before.

After being invited to a pool party, we were uninvited. When I decided we would bring Kyle, I was told it wasn't okay to come to this party. Some extended family members are uncomfortable around Kyle. He can be loud. His behavior is not typical. His differences are obvious. Some people find it difficult to know how to interact with him.

Kyle is capable of being at his best when outside the house. Even quiet. We have been working on helping him control his volume and he regularly astounds us with what he understands and can do. I know that many people simply aren't around him enough to know what's possible.

I've never been uninvited before. I felt a surge of emotion. Hurt, anger, sadness, rejection, yuckiness, frustration. Emotions often take up residence in the body, and these were settled in my gut.

At about the same time, I had been knee deep in noticing and exploring the incredible power of the energy of thought. This energy is kindling wood for the flames of emotion. Thought energy creates the personal movie in which we find ourselves. In my movie, my personal thinking and feelings felt like hail.

Quite loud and seeming justified were the self-righteous, mama bear thoughts of "how dare they?" I took it personally on Kyle's behalf. Then there was the continuous hum of judgments. "Really? After all these years, blah blah blah." Finally, a sharp punctuation of self recrimination blew in, "I shoulda, coulda, woulda helped people accept and really know Kyle."

I found myself analyzing. Disguised as questions, thoughts slipped in the back door of my awareness. "Don't I have the right to take this personally? Aren't my feelings justified? How is feeling miserable serving me? It's not but I will not give in. How can this be okay?" Hail, rain, drizzle. Ouch. Hail, rain, drizzle. Ouch.

After a while, I tried to will my mind to slow down and stop talking to me. On the edge of tears, I told myself to breathe, change the conversation, or distract myself. I'd had enough rain already. Feeling stuck, my thinking seemed to be clogging the pathways to inner peace. It looked like there was a permanent barricade on the road to seeing something different in this situation.

Twenty-four hours later, I found myself on the treadmill listening to music. Suddenly, something shifted within me. Without effort, my busy mind slowed down and I saw something I had not seen before.

I knew something brand new. This was not about me or Kyle. This was not about Kyle's value as a person. This was all about family members and their discomfort. It is common to run from the potential of future discomfort. There are times when we all do it.

It looks obvious to me now, but at the time, it was truly an a-ha moment. Words can't quite fully express what happened. In an instant, I saw something really big with every fiber of my being. This allowed me to experience compassion for my family. Without will or force, the rainstorm subsided. My gut relaxed. Effortlessly, it was now okay. Truly okay.

We feel our thinking. The good news is, our thinking is not reality. Similar to our nighttime dreams, it may appear real, until we wake up. It can feel wonderful or scary or awful just like a book or movie while we're engaged with it. In the end, we get to close the book or walk out of the theater. We know it's only a story.

And so it is with our personal thinking. Those thoughts are our stories. When they begin to slow down or dissolve, the book closes on its own and we experience something different. This shift may feel like a brand new way of seeing or being. There is a sense of a mental spaciousness, an opening. We may experience this as a deep feeling of peace or a new state of mind.

From this space, it's clear to me an umbrella was never necessary. My thoughts may hurt, but I could not be hurt by thought. I was always safe, always okay.

To realize it's your own creation ... your own misery is your own creation. That's pretty humbling. It changes everything to see that. How seriously can you take yourself in light of the fact that you're making it up?

—Jack Pransky, *Somebody Should Have Told Us:*
Simple Truths for Livng Well

BUBBLES

Your bubble, my bubble
Your reality, my reality
You see something, I see something else

My Son

Your thoughts project an image
that makes your picture of him
fuzzy or sharp
And scary perhaps
or
misty or clear
And beautiful perhaps

Your thoughts
Whether or not you know their specifics
fill your bubble
And create a reality

You act, based on that reality

Embrace, sit down, be with
Connect in the best way that comes to you
In the moment

or

Fear, walk away, look aside, shun
Disconnect, doing your best
In the moment

Your comfort zone is a formless boundary
The zone is not real or solid
just made of the energy of thought
You can walk through it
as you would a ghost
Or you can allow it to seal you
inside its fluid box

Appearing solid yet
Flexible and dissolvable
No zone to step outside of
Just a mirage made of the formless

Your thoughts bring you over
Your thoughts make you turn away

Your thoughts make your reality
Not the fact of autism
My son's behavior
My son

Bubbles

Sometimes our bubbles intersect
We have a common passion
A common perspective, similar thoughts
Then we see and feel our connection
It looks obvious, easy

Yes, we say
Yes, I get you and you get me
A little or a lot

Sometimes we stay separate in our bubbles
the tips of them touch
But maybe we go no further
Our separate realities feel so very separate

But still there is a connection
Our humanity
Like it or not
we are all connected to the same source
By our humanness
We plug into the same infinite intelligence
each night when we sleep
each day while awake

The connection
Invisible and powerful
like gravity and electricity

We get fooled by our separate realities
Yours should be like mine
Mine should be like yours
We forget we are wearing bubbles
Invisible
But constantly creating

Your reality
My Reality

Your bubble
My bubble

Slow-Motion Moments

THERE HAS ALWAYS BEEN a schism of sorts. A feeling of a divide in our family. Us and our girls. Us and Kyle. The girls and Kyle? Not so much.

This family dynamic was put in motion early on when Kyle's one-to-one therapy took place in his bedroom. Hours, days, and years ticked by. The girls were out having a life. Kyle's life was in his room. Small. There was a method to the madness that made sense for a while.

As years went on, it stopped feeling like the thing to do, and little by little, we introduced Kyle to the world and the world to Kyle. The kids are adults now. Kyle has a life outside his room. Thank goodness. His sisters, Rachel and Leah, are out on their own in different states, living their lives. Kyle still lives at home.

Leah is a singer, and Kyle listens to her music all the time. During a visit home, she decided to serenade Kyle. Despite a busy evening and last-minute guitar restring, she was determined to make it happen.

His birthday gift from Leah was a private concert at 10:30 PM. As a music lover, Kyle soaked it up. As a person with autism, his outer response was not immediately visible. But when she finished the first song, his grin was priceless.

A moment for Kyle, a moment for Leah, a moment for me. A precious moment in time where our connection felt palpable. Leah giving and Kyle receiving. Me, observing and feeling the sweetness that filled the room. The special energy of a string of slow-motion moments. Though I was exhausted, my soul felt energized.

It looks to me like the simplicity of the moment is where life's special elixir, the space of love, resides. Weeks later, I'm still smiling inside.

I was born the tree, and he the root.

—Leah Nobel, *Second and a Day* (song)

Discomfort

I'M NOT COMFORTABLE with _____.
Insert something. Anything. Lots of things.
How many times do we tell this to ourselves? And say this to others? Throughout the day, there are so many things about which to be uncomfortable.

How often do we allow discomfort, or the possibility of discomfort, to stop us in our tracks? We avoid taking action. Or having interactions and conversations. Or we take an action that we believe steers us away from discomfort. Only to find it around the next corner.

Or, we experience the anticipated discomfort, and ...

1. We see it's not fatal and there is no permanent harm done to self. In fact, we might even feel exhilarated afterward.

2. We muck around in it, like something gooey that is stuck to the bottom of our shoe. Feeling bad, we try to get rid of it. We keep feeling it anyway. Until we don't.

In fact, there is even a place we have designated as the comfort zone. We tiptoe around the edges of it as if a landmine exists on the other side.

Sometimes we accidentally (or purposely) step over the line, going outside the alleged zone. And hmmm, maybe nothing happens. Discomfort was not there after all.

The truth is, the line around this comfort zone is not real because it is made of the energy of thought. And at any moment, we are likely to think again and POOF! the zone changes.

And when we look a bit deeper, we may realize there is no zone. It is merely a figment of our imagination that may keep us from engaging fully in life.

For me, there have been many times where discomfort, or fear of discomfort, has kept me from following my intuition. Discomfort can be very noisy.

There have also been many times where I have simply plowed ahead despite the icky, yucky feeling of discomfort experienced in my mental and physical body.

It's easy to mistakenly believe the cause lies outside of us. A situation. A person. A thing. If only we could control or fix X, Y, or Z, then discomfort would vanish.

The truth is, nothing can MAKE us uncomfortable.

What?!? (Pssst, this is good news.) Discomfort is a result of the power of thought. Thought is energy and looks and sounds like ... personal thinking.

We experience thought as perceptions and feelings. And it creates our realities. It colors the lenses we wear. It literally creates each of our worlds.

We may hear it as chatter and stories in our head. It is associative in nature. One thought can lead to another. Pretty soon, we have innocently woven a fictional tale of woe. We latch on to it. And it certainly doesn't look fictional.

Hello, discomfort. Hello, worry about the possibility of future discomfort.

Thought also brews silently, beneath the surface of our awareness. Like a snowball, it picks up speed (more thoughts) as it careens down the hill of our consciousness. And suddenly we know we feel bad but might not have a clue as to what lurks beneath. We just feel that strong, unpleasant sensation of discomfort.

A few weeks ago, I knew I had to have an important conversation with someone. For days, every time I thought about it (or even when I didn't think I was thinking about it), I felt waves of discomfort. I imagined the other person reacting in a certain way. I imagined how they might feel. I did some mental gymnastics, justifying my point of view. The snowball got pretty big in the days leading up to the discussion.

Funny thing, when I stepped onto the stage of the conversation, even before I spoke, my thoughts seemed to fade, and discomfort dissolved. I said what I wanted to say. It was a two-second sentence. And to my surprise, the other person had the same opinion. Interestingly, that hadn't been part of my snowball.

I found myself in the moment. Talking, listening, responding. The conversation took on a life of its own. A flow. Dynamic and fluid. Out of my control.

Like life.

If the only thing people learned was not to be afraid of their experience, that alone would change the world.

—Sydney Banks

Knowing

THERE IS A POWERFUL FORCE within you and me. It's an energy that comes through as something that can be called *knowing*. We experience it as intuition, inner wisdom, a gut feeling.

Inner wisdom asks the questions and also provides the answers. They seem to spring from within. And also emanate from a force outside of us to which we are connected. They might appear to be triggered by something read, seen or heard. We might be guided to seek more knowledge or information by looking someplace specific or talking to someone.

Inner wisdom might be a nudge to get into motion and take action. Or it might be a stop sign that says to pause or wait. There is almost a hum to inner wisdom. It resonates.

There are no guarantees of outcome when we follow intuition. It's simply a signal that points us in a direction. It may or may not yield what we expect or desire. It directs us to the next place or step.

Personally, I've noticed my busy mind may try to think its way to another path. Pro and con noise creates a ruckus in my brain. But intuition keeps playing its tune, staying its ground and wanting to be heard.

Intuition nudges, taps me on the shoulder, whispers or even shouts. Without actually hearing specific words, I know something. "Go this way, try this, time to stop, don't decide now, here's the answer."

I recently had a powerful experience of knowing.

Kyle had been therapeutic horseback riding for almost twenty years. He was thirteen the first time we took him to the arena. Beforehand, I didn't really think it was for him. I had a long list of reasons why it wouldn't work. It took almost the entire half hour to get him on the horse that first session. Flanked by two side walkers and a horse leader in the front, there were only five minutes at the end where he got to ride. Although he was nervous and hung on for dear life, I could see the potential of a powerful connection there.

Each week that followed got easier. The volunteer staff, which included a certified instructor, as well as the horse, was infinitely patient with Kyle. It wasn't too long before Kyle began to mount the horse with ease and really enjoy riding. Eventually, with help, he could sit sideways, backward, or hang on for a trot. Kyle's joy and laughter while riding were delightful to watch.

Then during Kyle's nineteenth year of riding, he began to have difficulty mounting the horse. He would panic on the mounting platform, and no amount of coaxing or support seemed to help. Many evenings, we had to turn around and go home.

Other times, he was able to work through it. He was able to mount and ended up enjoying the ride. It looked like the issue was the mount rather than the ride, so we kept at it, showing up to the arena week after week. Getting creative, we tried new ways of supporting him. It wasn't time to give up.

Until I knew it was time to stop.

After a six-week break, his panic was more intense than ever. He was nervous even before approaching the stairs to the platform. Dad, who usually has the magic touch with Kyle, wasn't able to help him mount.

I could give it another try. Come back the following week and even the one after that. The staff was patient and left it to me. Even though I didn't want to hear it, my knowing had a clear message for me. Kyle doesn't want to do this anymore.

Is this knowing business that easy?

The decisions don't feel easy sometimes because my thoughts get involved. I loved that Kyle experienced the joy of riding a horse. So many years later, I still found my own joy in watching him. He had a special relationship with an animal who was so patient with him. I had a sense Kyle got more from it than we will ever know.

I was sad when I made the decision it was time for him to stop. A long and really special era was ending. But the knowing? That part was easy. Because I didn't have to do anything. Knowing comes naturally and is often experienced as a feeling. Even sadness didn't overpower it.

Knowing is part of the flow of life. And when I don't try to paddle against the current, the knowing takes me to the next place. It's both soothing and empowering at the same time.

"You'll know when you know" is one of my favorite mantras for myself. It's one I share with clients. So much less struggle and effort involved when we embrace it. Knowing feels like a sixth sense, a superpower.

We all possess this superpower. Sometimes we're asleep to it. Or we effort at rationalizing and talking over it. But it's always there. We can take off the ear muffs or set the blindfold down and we will sense the hum of intuition.

Then we know.

Knowing is a shift in one's level of understanding that cracks open the door of beliefs, and brings insight beyond habits of thought.
—Elsie Spittle, *Nuggets of Wisdom*

Hello, Wisdom

It wakes me up early in the morning
Flashing lights and loud gongs
The answer I need is clear and obvious

Wisdom
I am in awe of how the system works.
This wisdom business
This intuition, this knowing

Last night, I felt stuck, lost, worried
This morning I know exactly what to do
So clear, certain I am

I see steps 1,2,3,
No plans beyond that
And it's okay

I will figure it out in real time
On life's clock
"This is right," says wisdom "Very right"
"I know" I say "I know"

A song playing softly in the background
A light shining dimly, sometimes brightly
A feeling in my gut, or in my heart
Somewhere in my core

What I know without reasons to back it up
No pros, no cons
Just this

A powerful guidance system
At times it seems without logic or reason
It is what I know when I know

Hello wisdom
and
Thank You

Ability

KYLE GOES TO Ability 360, a gym for people with disabilities and their families. Being different is the norm here. It is more than okay. I can taste and feel the love and acceptance radiating from every corner of this place.

Serious sports are played at this gym. Recently, we were walking the raised track above the basketball courts. The track was practically vibrating with the energy below. Wheelchair basketball.

It was intense. It appeared serious and at the same time, fun. High energy, team sportsmanship, and athletic prowess filled the court. Athletes of various ages, and all in wheelchairs.

Spectators lined the perimeter of the court. As we walked, I found myself drawn in by the game below. The wheelchairs faded into the background. That nobody was on their feet became irrelevant. These guys radiated strength, passion, and vibrancy.

I wondered about the athletes and their stories. How did they come to be here despite not having full use of their legs?

How have they risen above what many would consider a huge athletic and life obstacle? What has it taken for them to put themselves in the game?

After interviewing a coach/player, I found out that wheelchair basketball is the oldest adaptive sport. When World War II veterans returned home, they needed something post rehabilitation. They were hungry for a physical and mental outlet.

Level of physical function is not a limitation for being a valuable team member. There is a weighted point system, so someone of any ability level is a plus to their team. Players are rated. With this system, the playing field is leveled and nobody is diminished for having less functioning.

With logistics taken care of, mindset can be the biggest obstacle. There might be hesitation about getting involved and perhaps fear, insecurity, and lack of confidence. These feelings may stop a person from showing up to play the game in the first place. Or from taking the first action or actions that follow.

It might look as if one would need a "work through it" strategy to fix, reframe, change or release a feeling or belief before wheeling out onto the basketball court. Is this true? Are certain feelings or state of mind necessary before taking action?

The good news is, no. This means there's so much less to do and nothing to fix. There are no prerequisites to taking the action of wheeling out onto the court. The freedom to compete, experience camaraderie, and have fun is always available.

Feelings, by themselves, do not have the power to control. Pregame insecurity or anxiety? It's possible to play anyway. Emotions are one of the incredible parts of being human. On their own timetable, they blow in and out like the wind. No person or situation can actually make us feel a certain way. Knowing this is so empowering.

Feelings originate from the formless energy of thought. Thought hums constantly beneath our awareness. Much of it passes through without attention. Some of it is brought to life by the movie maker, our consciousness.

Feelings and state of mind are the glasses we wear, constantly changing color, painting our individual realities, our experience of life. What if feelings don't matter? And rather than being insensitive or dismissive, this is empowering?

Feelings don't need to stop us. The players' thoughts/feelings don't have to keep them from showing up on the court. Despite what the world might define as a limitation, these players can play full out, participating to the best of their ability.

The athletes don't have to slay any emotional dragons or build confidence ahead of time to show up for the game. Action can serve as a framework for confidence.

Feelings are not inherently relevant. They are only as relevant as we make them, based on the attention we give them. We may not choose our thoughts and hence, our feelings, but we do get to choose our actions. We do get to choose whether we set our wheels in motion.

The state of mind of the athletes before they show up on the court is not necessarily what it will be in the moments that follow. Once they are on the court and in the flow of the game, a busy uncertain mind may slow, thereby creating space. Space for living in the moment and playing in the real time of the game.

One action at a time linked together, allowing the best of who they are to shine.

A B I L I T Y 360, all the way around.

People always tell you you're limited. It can control you or you can overcome it."

—Robert Reed, wheelchair basketball coach and participant

Feeling It

WE RECEIVE A LOT of messages from inside and outside ourselves about feeling happy and thinking positive. I was told early on if I could choose to be happy no matter what, I would be better for Kyle. If I could change my beliefs to the empowering positive ones, I would be in a strong position to help Kyle while at the same time feeling better within myself. It made sense at the time. Who wouldn't want to feel good most of the time, anyway?

The other extreme is the victim mentality of poor me, I got this child with autism. And poor boy, he has this condition called autism that hijacks his life. Feeling miserable and stressed is completely justified for all concerned. There are groups where whining and sympathizing are the main game. Going one step further, let's go to war with autism and figure out how to fix it so we can all feel better.

Being a victim of autism didn't resonate with me, so I went to the other extreme. For years, I explored personal growth strategies in search of the best paths to take for the ever elusive ideal emotional state. I worked hard at changing perspectives and beliefs, all the while advocating for Kyle like a mama bear. Sometimes I strained to change outside circumstances. At times, these strategies seemed effective, others not so much. It was always extra effort.

As I have begun to see the source of our emotions, I have noticed a shift in my relationship to them. Recently, I was wedged in next to Kyle in his recliner. He often finds this comfortable and comforting. At the time, he was extremely scared and needed a large dose of TLC. He was experiencing an intense reaction to a treatment we were experimenting with to help him during his cyclical agitation/anxiety episodes.

Honestly, I was pretty scared, too. I also noticed I was afraid of being scared. And on top of that, I was judging the fact that I was afraid of being scared. I may have also been judging the fact that I was judging myself for being afraid of being scared. Quite a few layers lurked beneath the iceberg.

Breathe? That didn't occur to me at the time, and I don't think I was doing any extra beyond what my body did automatically. If there were tools and techniques to shift my emotional state, they were not part of my awareness at that time.

My thoughts were like a loud internal windstorm. Lots of what ifs, should haves, what would I do ifs. Telling myself to calm down was not working to settle them. Asking myself what exactly I was really afraid of wasn't effective either. My mind was too full.

What if I sat with my fear rather than running from it or trying to analyze or fix it? Allow it, feel it and experience it. Notice where it hangs out in my body. That would be my gut. It was tight but not excruciating and certainly not life threatening.

Sit and be with what is showing up within me and in this space I share with Kyle. I sat with fear for a while. The thoughts were still singing their song but faintly in the background. I couldn't really hear them, but I could still feel fear so I knew they were still swirling beneath the surface of my consciousness.

At some point, I noticed other feelings took the place of fear. There was worry. An upgrade from fear. Worry eventually evolved into concern. Concern resulted in a softening. With that softening came compassion and getting in touch with love. And gratitude for being able to be there for Kyle and offer comfort. Tension drifted in and out. Doubt came and went.

Quietly, a feeling of confidence began to emerge. Well, hello there, confidence. Eventually, I regained a sense of my well-being, the default setting. In this moment of clarity, I felt something. A trickle of wisdom dripped in. I did what I knew to do, and this next action was rather simple. It was about patiently, calmly, lovingly waiting. Being present and sitting with Kyle where he was until the symptoms passed.

My emotional state became background noise as we connected soul to soul within a space of love. As I sat with Kyle, I sat with me. Where I was. Nothing to fix, change, or run from. After a while, without trying, I found myself breathing normally again.

In hindsight, I'm pretty sure I felt the full range of human emotions in a two-hour period of time. And for whatever reason, on that day, in those moments in time, that was exactly where I needed to be.

Emotions are the dance of our thoughts through our limbic system, transported back to our cerebral cortex via our senses to be experienced via another thought. The dance is ongoing and vibrant.

—William F. Pettit Jr., M.D.

Home

IT WAS ONLY 86 DEGREES and over-
cast here in Phoenix, Arizona, also known as
dry-as-toast land. Time to get out the door before the sun pokes
through the clouds. My dog pranced around, exuding cuteness
and enthusiasm when he saw my hiking boots.

It was my first day back.

Kyle had just come out of an intense 16-day cycle plus an
extra day at home to rebalance. I took a deep breath and exhaled.
We made it through another one. Sometimes thriving, sometimes
surviving. The full gamut of experience on the canvas of life.

As I trekked along on the trail, a strong sense of knowing
came to me. I was home. Home in that I experienced my well-being
again. Home in that I could smell, taste and feel peace of mind.
My outside circumstances were still not "perfect," and at the same
time, I felt perfectly okay.

I had a sense of who I am: a diamond on the inside, resilient
and creative. And although the winds of life had recently blown me

around quite a bit, I knew my feet were still firmly planted on the ground. The shiny diamond within me, my well-being, while caked with road dust, was still whole. And now it actually seemed visible.

I had a sense that no matter what, I am okay. And will be okay. I could see this for Kyle, as well. It feels like coming home. This insight washed over and through me.

Do I need the endorphins of exercise or the connection to nature to return home? Had I landed on a secret? It can appear this way. So taken with the fact that my sense of equilibrium had returned, I wanted to believe this was the definitive trick or tool to which I could turn next time I felt lost again.

That the road leading home is found by "doing stuff" is an alluring illusion. It's easy to get fooled. I've hiked with repetitive, negative, worried personal thinking, adding more dirt to my diamond. Home, obscured by thought storms swirling in darkened emotional skies.

Endorphins, while yummy, may be a side effect but not necessarily a cause of a shift in state of mind. There is no magic yellow brick road, and that's okay, too. From a state of clarity, I see that I am always one thought away from knowing home.

When you rest in the now, thoughts come and go, feelings come and go. Beneath all that comes and goes is a peace that is always here, always present.

—Dicken Bettinger & Natasha Swerdloff, *Coming Home*

Control: It's An Illusion

RECENTLY, WHILE PREPARING for a trip, I made a mega to-do list. The tasks ranged from quick and simple, requiring no brain power, to the lengthy, almost a project, lots of pre-planning, required-type stuff.

What is it with lists? Yes, a way not to forget a multitude of details and actions, especially before a trip. A way to remove thoughts from my head that can be distracting obstacles to creativity. Get it out of your head and onto the page, "they" say.

I've decided lists are also a tool for creating the illusion of control in my not-so-neat-and-tidy world. Maybe the brain gets a dopamine or serotonin hit when we check off those completed items. It feels soothing and satisfying.

After making my list, the first thing I did was rebel against it and do something else. Then I got a phone call. Then Kyle needed my attention. Eventually, I hacked my way through the list with lots of distractions and diversions as part of the game. Most of the items were completed by the end of the day. I didn't take this list game too seriously; hence, the inner and outer interruptions eventually became amusing to me.

I recently had an insight while working with a coach. It was about letting go of control. Doesn't the idea of letting go of control, even just a little bit, sound psychologically and spiritually wonderful? Something that could help us feel lighter and freer?

What I realized is I don't need to let go of control. There is nothing to let go of because control is an illusion. I never had it. I will never have it. Any thought, situation, or outcome masquerading as *in my control* is simply life lining up with what I desire. I understood this in a rock-the-way-you-have-always-seen-your-world, deeply insightful way.

Yes, sometimes and maybe I can have influence, but not control. I don't have control of situations, outcomes or other people. I don't even seem to have control of my thoughts. They appear and disappear randomly. Through my consciousness, I latch on to some of them or I don't. I can know not to take them too seriously. However, I can't even control whether I consistently do that, either.

I've decided this is good news. I can float down the river of life without kicking and screaming and resisting and paddling against the current. I might point my rudder in a certain direction (influence), but I know I may or may not get there. And whether I get there or not, the ride may be smooth or wild or a combination of both. When I forget I don't have control, I know I will eventually remember again and lighten up on the paddles.

If I never had control, there is nothing to let go of. Nothing to work on and nothing to do. Nothing to do? Nothing to do! Hey, that means there's one less item for my list. Hurray!

I can find only three kinds of business in the universe: mine, yours, and God's. ... Anything that's out of my control, your control, and everyone else's control, I call that God's business.

—Byron Katie

·

The Tea Shop

I HAD BEEN PART OF a program to create something that seemed impossible in ninety days. This was the impetus for writing this book.

There were a little over two weeks to go and I was sprinting toward the finish line. It wasn't likely I would get there in the time frame, but I had been showing up to write more often and for longer periods.

As I took next step after next step, I had a sense of my creative flow. Most of the time, I was playful rather than serious. I experienced less pressure and more enjoyment. I cared if I made the deadline, yet I didn't. I saw that it was arbitrary and part of the game. My timely completion would mean nothing about me. I knew I would eventually hold book in hand.

My laptop meandered about the house and I followed along. I seemed to write everywhere. An enjoyable place to write was also my neighborhood tea shop. It had an intimate, exquisite ambience. Soft music and the delicious aroma of teas mixed with the murmur of interaction between customers and staff.

One week I treated myself to two days of writing there. The first day, I experienced a magnificent flow. I sipped tea, allowing the words to slide out my fingers and onto the screen. A creative energy running full speed produced stories and poetry. It felt as if it was coming through me rather than from me. Ahh, the life of a writer.

The next day I returned, psyched for a similar experience. The magic seemed to be located in the gentle backdrop of the tea shop. However, what I experienced was completely different. I was distracted by almost everyone who walked in. I found myself drawn into listening to long conversations between staff and customers. I marveled at how people share so much of their life story while purchasing tea. I was amazed at how much money they spend. I coached people in my imagination. I daydreamed while gazing out the window.

The atmosphere of the tea shop seemed like the perfect tool for plugging into creativity. But all those people, they were distracting on the second day. Where had the magic gone? What happened to my writing flow?

In reflection, I can see I had a misunderstanding. I forgot there is no tool on the outside that can create our experience. Our experience comes from the inside, out, not the outside, in. It is 100 percent thought created. Even when we're unaware of the content of our thinking brewing beneath the surface, our experience is always generated by this amazing energy.

On the first day, my connection to my creativity felt like fluid motion. I heard the people in the shop, even interacted with them a few times, but I maintained a beautiful flow. Effortlessly.

On the second day, my mind was busy. Extraneous thoughts frequently interrupted my concentration. As much as I was aware of it and "trying hard" to stay focused, I had no control of my pesky thinking.

Taking a few deep breaths and admonishing myself to focus, I kept trying to slow my mind. In that moment it really looked like my experience was coming from outer distractions. If only the customers would stop coming in for a while. Or at least quit being so chatty and interesting.

It wasn't until I was driving home that I realized I'd been fooled again by the powerful energy of thought. It's the projector on the screen of our consciousness creating the movie called life. The movie making is fluid and seamless. And just like in a movie, we forget the projector is there.

But what about tools and techniques? A soothing tea shop, yummy cup of tea, or some long deep breaths.

When we stop and focus attention on our breath, our thoughts often slow and quiet. Afterward, we may experience a new clarity and calm. Rejuvenation. Fresh new thought replaces the old stale stuff. A space inside us seems to open and we feel more access to our creativity and well-being. A brand new state of mind.

Or we might stop and focus our attention on our breath because breathing is supposed to help settle the mind. Without realizing it, we might speed through the breaths in sync to our busy mind. Thoughts still racing and feeling tense, our state of mind stays busy. We might conclude that breathing doesn't really work for us.

Been there, done both.

I can show up at the tea shop and experience an amazing writing flow, convinced that this should be my new writing lair, only to discover the next day that the tea shop is the worst place for me to write. It's easy to see in hindsight that my experience wasn't created by the environment.

The power of thought always trumps tools and techniques. There may be a correlation and we may get innocently convinced it's a cause.

Tools and techniques are wonderful as long as I enjoy doing them. But they're not a doorway for me to experience my creativity. I've experienced my creative flow with the noise of Kyle in the background and frequent interruptions. I've had writing sessions alone in the house in dead quiet, yet experienced a busy, distracted mind. And vice versa for both scenarios.

The tools are optional. I've had a lifetime of playing around with them. I believed they were the key to thriving. But now I see they are an enjoyable option, not a necessity. This is because I have all that I need within me at all times. Knowing this, life just got simpler. And my to-do list (on paper or in my mind) just got shorter.

This might not seem like good news, but it is. There is no formula, technique, or tool that's required for creativity, focus, clarity, peace of mind, or well-being.

These are always within us. In fact, they are the fabric of us.

It turns out that we are the perfect judge of what is right for us when we are not looking for anything to be right for us. As we look inward we have a clear guidance that we can follow that has nothing to do with our changing thoughts and associated feelings. There seems to be a natural, easy, fun or interesting fit for us with certain people, certain activities, certain classes. There is that click or 'Yes!' or 'Found it!' that simply makes sense for us. This is where soulmates reside, lifetime fascinations and spiritual homes appear.

—Clare Dimond

Back to Normal

THE HOUSE IS SILENT. I take a deep breath. Tears of gratitude trickle out. It's been nearly two months since Kyle was seriously injured. He was a passenger when the car he was riding in, driven by a caregiver, was involved in an accident.

There is no boom of inner excitement or burst of joy. Nothing wild and celebratory is bursting forth from me. I experience a sense of relief and a quiet calm. Peace.

I note the wreckage in the kitchen and I don't care. Life, in all its messiness, is taking place in this house. I've decided I love the mess today and officially label it a good thing.

I take another deep breath. I hear from within me, "We are all okay now." Then, in an even quieter tone, without words, more like a sense or feeling, "And we always have been."

In my core, I know we have been okay the entire time. Beneath Kyle's broken bones, my worries and fears, living in the hospital for ten days, the surgery drama, the doctor and nurse drama, the caregiver drama, the rest, sleep, and exercise deprivation, was well-being.

Understandably, I lost touch with my sense of it. But like a tiny jewel, it sat deep within me. It was my power source for connecting with deeper intuition and wisdom.

Back to normal? I have a sense that I am. But not really. Because my normal will never be the same as the normal before the night I received the phone call about the accident.

"We've been hit. He came out of nowhere. Kyle's nose is bleeding. We are at the intersection down the street."

That was it.

My husband and I both assumed it was a fender bender and we would be picking Kyle up to drive him home. We arrived to a scene of crunched metal and emergency vehicles. Miraculously, a couple who have two children with autism happened to stop at the accident scene. The mother was talking calmly to Kyle through the open car window.

The me of two months ago is not the same as the one I know today. I got tossed out of my comfortable life boat into some really cold, choppy water. It was very startling.

Each time I felt pushed below the surface, I eventually popped up again. Surviving and even thriving, I experienced my resilience, a beautiful feature of the human design.

I also had a new sense of my connection to inner wisdom. This is a powerful guide that comes through as intuition. Sometimes I didn't hear it. Sometimes I didn't listen. But it was always there, yelling, nagging, whispering, nudging, waiting.

Back to normal? I'm questioning the concept as well as my insistence on wanting it.

What if normal is a myth and the idea of getting back to it is simply a resistance to feeling a certain way? Or having to deal with certain things? A strong desire for life to be as it was before. A desire to flow in the same stream, feeling and caring about the same things in the same way as in the past.

What if normal is right here where I am now? And in all the moments to come? Not in some past that only exists in my memories, my thoughts. It looks to me like the more I strain toward normal in my mind, the less I notice what's right in front of me.

Going back to life as it was before the accident suddenly feels stale. Like eating leftovers that are a couple of days past their prime. Why would I want to do that when I can look to the oven and pull out a pan of fresh, hot, bubbly food—perhaps with some new ingredients and spices.

As I sort this out, I see there really isn't anything to get back to. The past is in my mind, my thoughts. There's only what's right here. And what comes next and next and next.

The puzzle pieces of my life and who I am have been reshuffled and set out on a blank canvas. Some are missing, some are new and many sit askew or upside down, waiting to be assembled to create something fresh.

Squinting, I begin to see a new picture ... normal.

Through the centuries, the wise have told us to live in the now. This is why I say to you ... The past is a ghost that cannot be held in the palm of your hand. The future cannot be grasped, no matter how desirable or enticing it may appear. Nor can the present be held, no matter how beautiful or exciting.

—Sydney Banks, *The Missing Link*

Will It Happen to Me?

NOBODY WISHES AHEAD OF time for a child with autism. "Please let my child be healthy" is the prayer said most often. If there is autism in the family, a whisper, "Please don't let my baby have autism."

When Rachel was a little girl of around four, she asked if I thought she could someday have a child with autism. In her four-year-old mind, she noted how I had a brother and son with autism, and she had a brother with autism, so that must mean she may one day have a son with autism. Beyond the answer "maybe," I don't remember the rest of what I told her. The reality of it appeared to be a million miles away.

My daughters, Rachel and Leah, are now thirty-one and twenty-nine. We have floated in and out of the "Will it happen to me?" conversation over the years. I'm also guessing it has been on their minds more than I know. Genetics, as advanced as it has become, still doesn't have much information for us.

It looks to me like we overthink the possibilities, creating worry and fear, until we're emotionally exhausted. The thoughts pass, and we settle. And then, we repeat the process.

Looking in from the outside, having a child with autism looks different to different people. When it's your brother, you experience it filtered through your own thoughts as a sibling. You observe your parents and draw conclusions.

My experience as a mom to Kyle was completely different from my mother's experience with my brother. Different generation, different me, different son. Taking it one step further, different thinking, different choices, different actions.

As a mom, I want to protect my daughters from heartache and difficulty. I want them to have what they want. I want life to be smooth sailing, certainly less bumpy than mine. Then I remember I'm not in control of their experience. Their journey will not be their grandmother's, nor mine, but very much their own.

The space of love they will share with their yet-to-be-born child can't be felt or understood from where they now sit. Though one may try, it's impossible to accurately imagine the experience of becoming a mother for the first time. There's an indescribable magic in that space.

What I really want my girls to know is, no matter what, they will fall in love with that little soul from the first moment they set eyes upon him or her. Their hearts will be forever stolen. Brand new life. There's nothing quite like it. Mother and child, a relationship like no other.

If they discover that soul has autism, he or she will still be their love. It will not feel anything like their relationship with their brother. They might have times when their heart may feel like it cracks, but those cracks will heal stronger. Love will become rocket fuel for the journey. The truth is, no one can know what it's like ahead of time to be mom to a child with autism. Like life, it is experienced moment to moment, in real time.

I know these things for sure, yet these words may not be much comfort. My girls will have their own experience, their own learning, their own insights. I sometimes forget I can't protect them from fear, heartbreak, sadness, and struggle. And really, why would I want to? These feelings are a fluid part of the human experience.

I trust their resilience. I know, at their core, they are strong and okay even when they, themselves don't feel it. I know they will do the best they can and they will rise in ways they can't possibly predict. I know they have access to the wisdom they need for each unique situation.

Will it happen to me? Maybe yes, maybe no. Without knowing what life is sending around the next corner, I do know that whatever happens, I will be there for them. My love will be shining in full force, supporting them and knowing my girls have all they need within them to live their lives. And live them well.

Between stimulus and response there is a space. In that space is our power to choose our response. In our response lies our growth and our freedom.

—Viktor E. Frankl

The Letter

ONE OF THE BIGGEST challenges we face as parents of kids on the autism spectrum is planning and preparing for the time when we will no longer be here to care for our children. Due to the special needs of many people with autism, this is true no matter the age.

Who will take care of our child or adult? What is the desired living situation? Will they be treated with love, patience, kindness, and respect? Who will make decisions on their behalf? Or support them in making decisions? Look out for their well-being in all areas? Who will continue to help them be the best they can be? Who will care when we are no longer here to care? The list can get long.

The questions feel big. Especially for parents, like myself, who don't yet have this figured out. Each question seems to open the door to a gust of emotions.

Kyle needs full-service care, from shaving to meal preparation to life decisions and everything in between. Someone to care deeply about him and love him would be nice, too.

Others with autism can live independently yet need a level of supervision and support. Many people are somewhere in between. Our kids on the autism spectrum have needs that are above and beyond and some, even hidden. They are vulnerable.

I'm working on a letter of intent. I'm actually revising the one I wrote four years ago. It feels like a big deal. At the moment, it looks no easier to create than it was back then.

Letter of Intent. Week after week, these words have adorned my To-Do list. Yes, I nod. I need to write that letter. And then I move on to something else. Something I don't fear as much. Something that looks easier. Sigh.

When I opened the one I wrote four years ago, I saw that so many things have changed since then. Note to self. Revise this letter more often. I copied the old letter into a fresh document. No point in completely reinventing the wheel.

I get out my binoculars and attempt to peer into the future. What do I see for Kyle when my husband and I are not here to make him a great life? I squint, trying to make the picture clear. Adjust the lens. Still nothing. Just a blur. Dang binoculars. They don't work for looking into the future. Especially into a future where I am no longer in the picture.

I remember I can't predict the future. Well, duh. But maybe I can plan for the future. Yes, I can come up with something. There's no guarantee that a shred of it will come to being. But I can certainly state my wishes. Which are? In some areas, unclear to me at this moment.

Suddenly I know that everything will be okay. I am okay. He is okay. All will get figured out when it needs to be, which is in real time. There are people close to Kyle who will step up on his behalf. I will state what I want and worry less about the how.

Still, I feel stuck and notice I'm pressuring myself. My fingers hover over the keyboard. Too many questions, not enough answers. My answers will be best guesses. Is that enough? Discomfort, judgment, and fear fog my glasses, clouding my vision.

Breaking through my internal noise, I eventually hear a whisper from within, a glimmer of insight. "Write from where you are right now. Give it your best and see what comes to you. Don't try to predict the future. What do you know to be true in this moment? Consult your heart."

I notice myself breathing again. That helps. I can only write what I know. There will be a lot of things to figure out that I can't plan for from where I sit in this moment. That's part of the game. The future without me will be different than any future with me here. This is hard to wrap my head around.

I begin to comb through the details of the document. And when I get to the part about where he'll live and who will do the day-to-day care, I stop. I don't know.

Soon ideas come. There are a few options. I don't love them, but I do my best to explore possibilities.

The future looks fuzzy. As much as humans try to predict and control the future, it can't be done. Especially when we're planning for our children. Life has a way of changing and moving at its own speed. It's difficult to corral into a plan. Whether we like it or not, a plan must be fluid, even on paper. The future lives only in our imaginations.

Another whisper. "Do your best. Be okay with not knowing." The ultimate in letting go. The unknown is the place from where new possibilities emerge. Write something that is good enough. Sit with it. Maybe even ask for help.

What I come to see is that as long as there is love and money available for Kyle, the details, with the help of those around him, will be worked out. Like life, this plan will be a work in progress. It can only be this way.

In my mind, the Letter of Intent will not go into effect for a very long time. At least that's my plan. And by that time, I will have Kyle situated in a living situation that I have created. So there will be less to figure out for the people in his life. I will have revised the letter many more times. However, since one never knows, I write the letter as if it will go into effect tomorrow. I have to set the binoculars aside, remembering they don't work for tomorrow, either.

I keep writing. Tears are allowed. Feelings are allowed. I stay with the writing. I write from where I sit and what I see in this moment. It's okay if it doesn't feel good to write this letter. I don't have to orchestrate an ideal mindset here. That's not possible, anyway. Thoughts, feelings, and attitude will come and go. Fluid. Like life. Not my job to fix them.

Uncertainty sings a soft melody in the background. A little noise in the system. I can still do what I know to do. Keep going. See where the flow takes me.

As I write, words filling the page, I begin to settle. Something shifts. I see that I can do this. And I do.

Out of nothing everything dances into existence.
　　　　　　　　　　　—Dicken Bettinger & Natasha Swerdloff, *Coming Home*

Amazing Design

I'T'S NOT MY JOB to beat my heart. I can exercise to keep it strong, but it's going to work without me. I can go hours, days, weeks and months without even thinking about my heart. It still works because that's part of the human design.

It's not my job to aid my lungs in breathing. I may want to take some deliberate deep breaths because it feels good. But my lungs will keep on contracting and expanding without my help. They will step it up during exertion. Truly amazing.

It's not my job to assist my kidneys and liver in doing their jobs. I can drink lots of water and eat healthily, but they are still on their own. They filter the good stuff and the junk. They keep functioning without my assistance.

It's not my job to grow the tree outside my front door or tell it when to drop its messy bulbs and leaves. I can support it by feeding and watering, but after that, it does quite well on its own. Even in the wicked Arizona heat, it knows what to do.

It wasn't my job to orchestrate the development of the three babies we created. Build arms, legs, fingernails, hearts, lungs, brains. Like the tree, food and water are important. But after the initial planting of the seed, the innate design of a developing baby is not up to me. I'm not in charge, thank goodness.

My heart, my lungs, my kidney and liver, a tree, my babies are all plugged into an innate universal intelligence, a grand design that enables the systems to work on their own. Each seems to come with its own built-in kit.

So given this powerful intelligence behind life, maybe it's not my job to attempt to orchestrate and micromanage the future. Or to strain and worry myself to solutions. And pre-plan conversations and a million next steps to get someplace. Now I see clearly that it isn't my job to control or fix my thinking, moods, and feelings. That's a big one.

There is a job for me. It's much simpler than I had imagined.

To flow with life, steering the boat when I can, but knowing that ultimately, I'm not in charge of the current or even getting to the destination.

To understand that my experience comes from the inside out, rather than the outside in. And when I forget, to notice when I remember again.

To allow my ever-transient thoughts and feelings to flow through, exercising the choice to act or not act on them but otherwise let them come and go.

To notice and rely on resilience, the innate ability of myself and others to bounce back.

To ride the wave of life, knowing I will be okay because I am okay. My children will be okay because they are okay. What life piles on can't hurt our solid core. Well-being lives beneath circumstances and feelings.

To know deeply that I can't and don't have to fix myself, my children, my husband or anyone else. Not even autism.

To show up to life, listen to wisdom when I hear it or feel it, and take the next step, and then the next.

To remember I'm connected to the force that makes babies and trees and all the complicated systems that comprise humans. A force that is both outside me and within me yet is so much larger and more powerful than myself.

The force behind the amazing design.

Additional Reading

The Missing Link: Reflections on Philosophy and Spirit, 1998, 2018 by Sydney Banks

The Enlightened Gardener, 2001, 2016 by Sydney Banks

The Path to Contentment, 2018 by Elsie Spittle

The Relationship Handbook: A Simple Guide to Satisfying Relationships, 2017 by George Pransky

The Inside Out Revolution: The Only Thing You Need to Know to Change Your Life Forever, 2013 by Michael Neill

The Space Within: Finding Your Way Back Home, 2016 by Michael Neill

Aha!: How to Solve Any Problem in Record Time, 2016 by Mary Schiller

The Joy Formula: The Simple Equation That Will Change Your Life, 2016 by Mary Schiller

Mind Yoga: The Simple Solution to Stress that You've Never Heard Before, 2016 by Mary Schiller

The Heart of Thriving: Musings on the Human Experience, 2017 by Kimberly Hare

Coming Home: Uncovering the Foundations of Psychological Well-being, 2016 by Dicken Bettinger and Natasha Swerdloff

One Thought Changes Everything, 2017 by Mara Gleason

Somebody Should Have Told Us!: Simple Truths for Living Well, 2011 by Jack Pransky

Do Nothing to Get Everything, 2013 by Amir Karkouti

Real: The Inside Out Guide to Being Yourself, 2018 by Clare Dimond

3 Principles Movies/Animations http://www.threeprinciples movies.com

Thinking in Pictures: My Life with Autism, 2008 by Temple Grandin

The RDI Book: Forging New Pathways for Autism, Asperger's and PDD with the Relationship Development Intervention Program, 2014 by Steven Gutstein

AUTISM–Behind The Locked Door: Understanding My Life as an Autistic, 2017 by Paul Louden

Fall Down 7 Times Get Up 8: A Young Man's Voice from the Silence of Autism, 2017 by Naoki Higashida

ACKNOWLEDGMENTS

*S*PACE OF LOVE began with a seed in the form of a question. If you knew there was a 20 percent chance or less of creating something you really wanted to create, would you go for it anyway? This question was proposed by transformative coach Michael Neill in the beginning of his 90-day course, Creating the Impossible. I am grateful to that seed and to Michael for the inspiration to begin writing this book.

With deep appreciation for Sydney Banks, who I never had the opportunity to meet. His enlightenment experience and then teachings in the form of books, videos, and audios uncovered the simple, yet profound understanding of the human experience known as The Three Principles. This was a life-changing gift that led to many powerful insights as it connected me in a profound way to a deeper spiritual understanding.

I am most grateful to the coaches and mentors I have worked with and learned from directly in the Three Principles community: Sara Murre, Mary Schiller, Kimberly Hare, Dr. William

Pettit, Dr. Linda Pettit, Natasha Swerdloff, Barbara Patterson, and Rohini Ross.

I am deeply grateful and appreciative of Kyle's team: Tammy Kenyon, Wendy Heredia, Angelica Ortiz, Sara Walton, Kim Isaac, and Fatima Nasr. Their support, dedication, and love shared so generously with Kyle and our family allowed me the space of time and mental bandwidth to even consider writing another book. A special thank you goes to Tammy for tirelessly listening to me talk about this book, reading the very rough draft, and letting me know I was on to something special.

With appreciation to the *Space of Love* creation team:

Mary Schiller, editor, for her honesty, patience, encouragement, and fine eye for detail as well as true understanding of the message within this book.

Christy Moeller, cover designer, for her patience and creativity as she captured the essence of this book so quickly and beautifully.

Michele DeFilippo and her team at 1106 Design, for going another round with me as interior designer, typesetter, proofreader, cheerleader and hand holder.

Sylvia Nobel and her publisher, Nite Owl Books, for support, encouragement, and push to complete this book so we could partner up in getting it out to the world.

I am grateful for:

My dear friend and previous coauthor, Kathy Almeida, who has been encouraging and supporting my writing for the last twenty-seven years. It was Kathy who helped me realize I had something to say and who inspired me to write the first words way back when. A special thank you for walking this autism walk with me.

Carrie Bell, author and friend, who has been a cheerleader for this book every step of the way and inspires me with her own writing, life insights, and courageous attitude in the face of big life challenges.

Robin Asaki, long-time friend, for her support, encouragement and keen eye for detail.

Lana Bastianutti, long distance friend, for her support, encouragement, and jumping in at the last minute for a final proofread.

With special love and gratitude for:

My daughters Rachel and Leah, who inspire me, each in their own unique ways, with their humor, common sense, creativity, deep insights, and zest for life. They have both been my rays of sunshine during many a dark moment, teaching me more than they could ever imagine, as well as giving me the opportunity to be a regular mom.

My husband, Neil, for believing in me with his endless support, encouragement, kindness, respect and love. His humor has been a beautiful reset button for our journey with each other and with our children.

Kyle, one of my greatest life teachers. *Space of Love* would not be here without him and the lessons I continue to learn as his mom. I am so grateful to be able to share this story.

About the Author

G AYLE NOBEL has a life-long connection to autism through her brother and son. She holds a BA in special education and is currently a transformative life coach, parent mentor, blogger, and inspirational speaker. *Space of Love* is her third book on living with autism. Gayle resides in Phoenix, Arizona, with her husband and son. Gayle can be found online at www.gaylenobel.com

Photo: Dana Gibbons

As an Introduction to
Gayle Nobel's previous books
on living with Autism
We invite you to preview
THE FOLLOWING BONUS CHAPTERS

IN

It's All About Attitude

&

Breathe

Published by
Nite Owl Books
and
Desert Beach Publications
Phoenix, Arizona

Print and e-Books are available through
most retail book outlets and online bookstores.

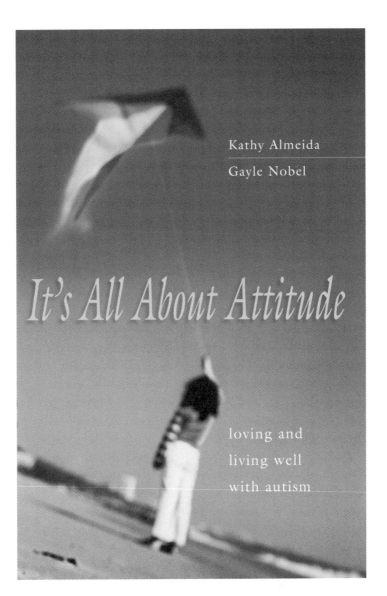

Kathy Almeida

Gayle Nobel

It's All About Attitude

loving and
living well
with autism

Serendipity

Gayle

I met Sarah in the bookstore by sheer coincidence. I was in line, waiting for help, and heard her ask the clerk for help locating books on autism. She was obviously still raw from her son's brand new diagnosis because when I told her that I, too, had a son with autism, the tears came easily.

I immediately had a strong desire to give her something, and I knew it had to be more than the latest intervention to try or book to buy. What could I offer, in that moment, knowing I might never have contact with her again? I wanted to sum up eighteen years of experience and share some profound words of wisdom. So, with a sense of urgency, I fumbled for words: "Though I know it doesn't seem like it right now, your little boy is an amazing gift to you. Not the one you expected, but one that will change your life and transform you in remarkable ways." Now we were both teary eyed.

As it turned out, this serendipitous meeting with Sarah transformed me as well. By reflecting on Sarah's questions, I was able to gather together what I had learned—the things that had made a difference for me over the years—and record them. In the week that followed, I wrote Sarah a long letter, a mini-guidebook of sorts. Kathy and I had just begun writing this book, so in many ways, this letter became my outline and writing guide.

In the months that followed, Sarah and I became friends. Through supporting Sarah, I lifted myself up as well. In answering her questions, I became inspired to live those answers. As I shared with Sarah, I taught myself, once again, the keys to feeling good, living well, and making a difference for Kyle. I became stronger and more confident as I relearned my own lessons.

One of the many pivotal questions Sarah asked was, "What would you do differently if you had it to do over?" As I explored this, I realized how amazing hindsight is. Everything was much clearer to me now, looking back with my accumulated wisdom and experience. It was not as easy to see the best path back then, faced with different choices, each with its own unique challenges.

With the perspective of hindsight, there are many things I wish I had done differently. However, for each of those things, there is also a reason I am grateful for what I did. There was simply no way to know beforehand what would be effective. Perhaps I kept Kyle at home for too long, isolating him. However, our home program was an illustration of my dedication and commitment to what I believed was right at the time. Maybe it was also an example of my stubbornness, possibly born out of fear. There are always two sides to everything.

Mistakes have turned out to be great teachers, sometimes proving to be even more helpful than "success" would have been. At times, those mistakes spurred new ideas or motivated me to open my mind and explore other options that might benefit Kyle. And, while some of the specific techniques we used didn't really work for him, our attitude of love, acceptance and gratitude became our foundation, infusing all our interactions with gentle compassion. With great love and respect, we strived to give him the "you are doing the best you can" benefit of the doubt. We endeavored to let go of judgments about his behavior and autism as a whole. We looked for things to celebrate, no matter how miniscule, wanting to focus on what was, rather than what wasn't. If I could do things over one hundred times, I would not want to change those things.

Though it's easy to look back and make mental corrections or judgments, I'm not sure how useful this is. In answer to Sarah's question about what I would have done differently, I now believe that wherever I chose to go was where I was meant to be—part of a divine plan I didn't, and don't, control.

A random meeting in a bookstore was a meaningful event on this journey. In helping Sarah, I was able to help myself. Call it coincidence, serendipity, or even divine intervention, it was most definitely a gift.

Connections

Gayle

After being sick for a week, Kyle rebounded by having an amazing three days. I was delighted and excited, wishing I could freeze the moments, making them last forever.

There was an awareness and attentiveness about Kyle I don't often see. At times, it was almost magical. Kyle was very active, but not hyperactive or out of control. He appeared more interested in people and his surroundings than usual. He wasn't attracted to his routine, repetitious activities. Several times, I found him just standing in his room, or in the hallway, waiting for something to happen with a distinct and unusual clarity, alertness, and focus. He seemed more organized, his neurological system allowing him to follow through on routines with ease.

I find these times fascinating and mysterious. I have created visual images—metaphors—to help me understand something I find baffling. Kyle's mind reminds me of an electrical cord plugged into an outlet. When he is "on," it's as if the synapses in his brain are connecting and firing fully. The cord is plugged in and the current is powerful, strong, and continuous. Kyle is able to perceive the world more clearly because many of the riots and distractions that normally fill his brain are quiet.

I imagine during other, more typical, times, his brain is filled with static. While it is plugged in, the electrical cord is not completely pushed into the socket. It's loose and jiggling around so the connection is sometimes complete and sometimes not there at all, but most often is fuzzy and irregular. The connection comes and goes like a radio signal fading in and out, mixed with interference.

What must it be like to experience the world through Kyle's senses? In the blink of an eye chaos replaces calmness. The patterns he relies on are abruptly removed. Trying to make sense out of it all, he seeks familiarity, sameness, and consistency in a world that is spinning rapidly around him.

Yesterday morning, when Kyle awoke, the plug was almost completely free of the outlet. I could see that the prior days' connection had vanished. Here was a Kyle who didn't quite have his act together. This became apparent right away when I noticed the look in his eyes, heard the sounds he was making, and observed the way he navigated through his morning routine. The window of opportunity experienced during the prior days appeared closed.

We all have our off days. Nobody is completely consistent each day, though Kyle's ups and downs are often more extreme. It's as if someone keeps tripping over that electrical cord and disengaging it. Often, I look for a reason for the variations. Was it something we did? A food he ate? The weather? An illness or allergy? The full moon? Rarely do I have any answers. On any given day, the plug will engage and the window of opportunity will again present itself.

I realize that if I am to exist happily and peacefully, I must strive to live more in the present moment, learning to love the times when the plug is loose and the cord is dangling. Anyone can delight in the extraordinary moments. I strive to embrace the more challenging times that bring the tougher lessons. It is an ongoing process.

Each morning, I wake up to a surprise at the other end of the house. It is Kyle's ever-evolving way of being. One day at a time, we both grow and transform. Kyle takes on his challenges with amazing grace. As for me, I strive to do the same.

BREATHE

52 Oxygen-Rich Tools for Loving and Living Well with Autism

GAYLE NOBEL

Coauthor of *It's All About Attitude: Loving and Living Well with Autism*

Photography by Rachel Nobel

MOMENTS

I got a phone call from my husband, Neil. It went something like this:

"Have you started dinner yet?"

"Just starting it."

"I would like to take you and Kyle out to dinner to celebrate the end of the month."

Though dinner was partially started, I jumped at the opportunity.

It was late. It was at least an hour and a half past Kyle's usual dinnertime. The restaurant we chose – one that Kyle enjoys and is familiar with – turned out to have a very long wait, so we decided to go somewhere else. This is not so easy for someone with autism. Kyle got excited just walking across the parking lot, but we had to switch gears and turn around. He went with the flow.

Thinking fast, we remembered the new gluten-free pizza restaurant across the street. It, too, was crowded, and there were no booths available to provide the structure so helpful to Kyle. Instead, we were seated at an awkward metal table outside with the traffic noise, lots of lights in the background, and a crying baby, where we waited for our food. Kyle handled the uncertainty and obstacles with grace. He remained quiet and relatively calm.

We stayed calm too, and even ventured into the realm of typical dinner conversation.

We were having a moment.

Satiated with gluten-free pizza, it was time to leave. The patio was now packed, and I knew how much Kyle wanted to run. He rose to the challenge of getting up slowly. I followed along as Dad confidently guided him through the narrow maze of people and food-filled tables. Kyle calmly followed. My two guys were at their best.

From beginning to end, this was an evening of moments.

For many families, having an easy dinner on Friday night is probably typical and taken for granted. For us, it was anything but typical, and we certainly didn't take it for granted. This was the first time it didn't feel "hard" to be with Kyle in a restaurant. Dining out as a threesome was actually enjoyable and comfortable.

I thought about what brought us to this place in time. There were so many roadblocks and unexpected twists and turns. How did we get here? There was no magic formula; just persistence, I suppose. Believing in more than what we could see. Trusting ourselves, yet also allowing others to teach and help. Growing in our own roles as guides in the school of relationships and life, as Kyle grew as apprentice.

And, watching for those moments.

Oxygen-Rich Tool

Watch for your moments. They will come. Moments pack an extra punch when you share them with someone, so pick up the phone.

SILENCE

Last night, we sat on the stone wall in front of our house. This is one of Kyle's favorite places to sit after taking a walk, and part of our regular routine. We take in the night air, the moon, and the scent of the fragrant desert plants. We also take in each other. I might make an occasional comment, and Kyle, an occasional sound, but nearly always, we sit in silence.

There is space in the silence. In this space, I notice. I notice my son, and how much he enjoys the simple things in life. I notice his reactions, and his thinking moments, which can be subtle and easily missed. I feel the strong connection between us. I am reminded that to connect with another person is not just about the words that go back and forth. Connection is the unspoken, invisible part of the relationship between two people. It lives in the body language, facial expression, attitude, and, most importantly, the way those people intertwine in the dance that is a relationship.

It's taken me a long time to fully appreciate these moments of silence. I've had to learn to turn off the voices in my head that tell me I "should" be doing something more, like using this as a teachable moment. The list of things I should be doing is endless. Should be, should be, should be. It's also a distraction, because it diverts my attention from the moment, from what is.

I hear Kyle's heart and soul in the sound of the silence between us. As the artist, Allison Krauss, sings so beautifully, "you say it best, when you say nothing at all."

Oxygen-Rich Tool

Savor the silence with your child, or someone else you love. What do you notice? What do hear in the silence?